Marsha McCloskey's

FEATHERED · STAR QUILT · BLOCKS · I

Ten Favorite Le Moyne-Based Stars

Really Hard Blocks That Take a Long Time to Make

INTRODUCTION

Are you ready to make Feathered Stars? If the answer is "yes," it means that:

- You are an experienced quiltmaker with good piecing skills.
- You can cut and sew accurately.
- You are not afraid of tiny pieces.
- You have experience with set-in, partial and curved seam piecing.
- Once you have a block made, you can design a quilt to go around it.
- You are not in a hurry.

Some of the block patterns in this book are really hard and take a long time to make. Other designs are fairly straightforward.

Geometrically, there are two categories of Feathered Stars: Le Moyne-based stars and grid-based stars. The ten Feathered Star block designs in this book are all based on the Le Moyne Star. A Feathered Star based on a Le Moyne Star will have equidistant points tipped with diamonds, and the number of Feather triangles along each side of the star legs will be the same. These diamond-based block designs have been called the "true" Feathered Stars.

The other group of Feathered Stars are based on Sawtooth or Variable stars. These grid-based stars are characterized by points that are not equidistant, and usually have a large square in the center. The Feather triangles of grid-based stars need to be drafted in two different sizes to fit properly and the tips are parallelograms instead of diamonds. These stars will be included in a second book called *Feathered Star Quilt Blocks II: Best of the Grid-Based Stars*.

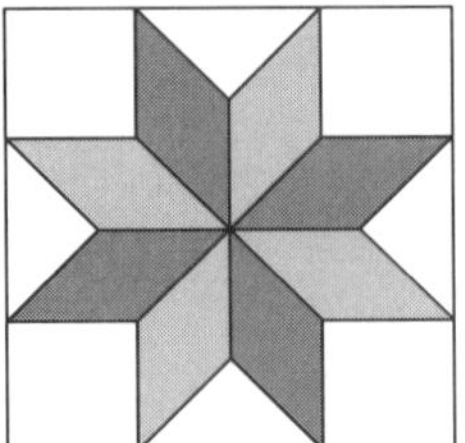

Le Moyne Star

Le Moyne-based Feathered Star

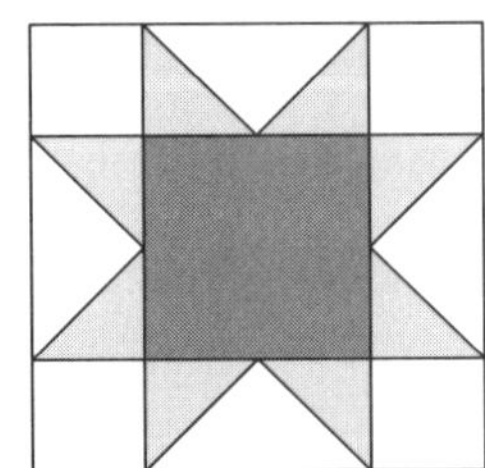

Grid-based Sawtooth Star

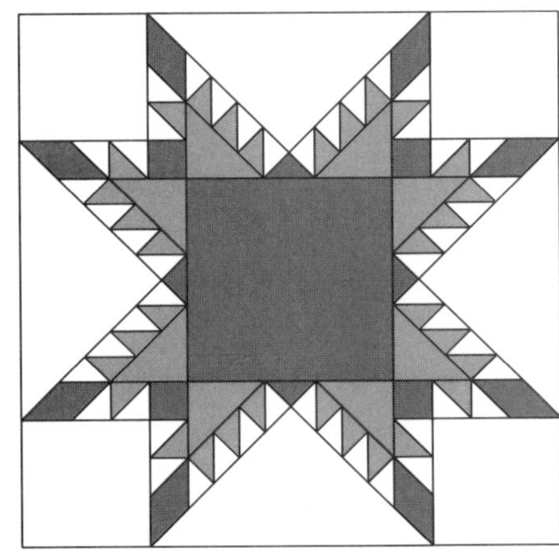

Star of Chamblie: Grid-based Feathered Star

DRAFTING

If you don't like drafting, skip this section. But, if you want to know how these stars really work, try these exercises. Drafting lets you get inside a design and truly know it. It is one of my favorite things about quiltmaking.

Supplies

- 17" x 22" sheets of ⅛" graph paper with heavy lines at the 1" increments
- Sharp pencil and eraser
- Drawing Ruler – C-Thru B-85 (2" x 18" clear plastic with ⅛" grid printed in red)
- Bow Compass with a 7" radius
- Colored pencils

Le Moyne Star

I use this drafting method often to make different star designs for the centers of the Le Moyne-based Feathered Stars. The basic Le Moyne star has three shapes: a diamond, a square, and a triangle. The geometry of the star is unique in that all the sides of the diamond are equal to all the sides of the square, which are equal to the two short sides of the triangle. It can be drafted on graph paper or plain unlined paper. These directions apply to any size square.

1. Draw a square on a sheet of paper.
2. Draw two diagonal lines to divide the square in half, both ways. Where the two lines cross is the center of the square. Draw two more lines, one vertically and one horizontally to further divide the square into 8 equal triangles.

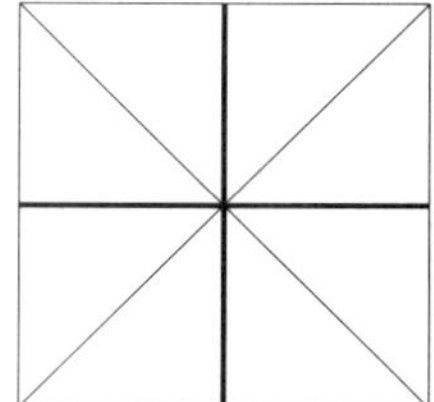

3. With a compass, take a setting diagonally from the center of the square to one of its corners. Keeping this dimension, move the point of the compass consecutively to each corner of the square, making two marks from each corner on each side of the square. These marks locate the 8 points of the star.

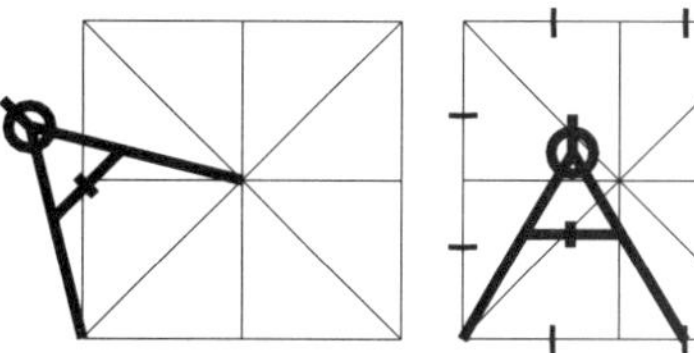

4. Draw four lines to join the points vertically and horizontally across the square.
5. Draw four more lines joining the points diagonally across the square.

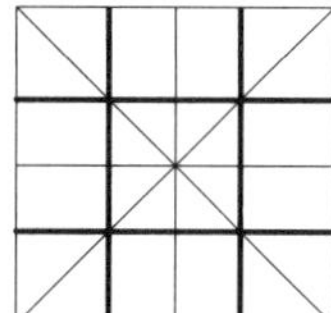
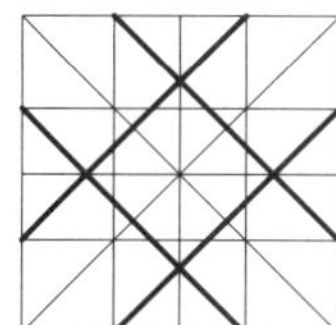

6. Find the diamond, square and triangle that will be templates and color them in with a colored pencil. ***Note:*** Study the lines you have made. You could make many different stars based on this set of lines. Add a few more lines and the possibilities multiply.
7. Add ¼" seam allowances around each colored shape to find cutting dimensions or make templates.

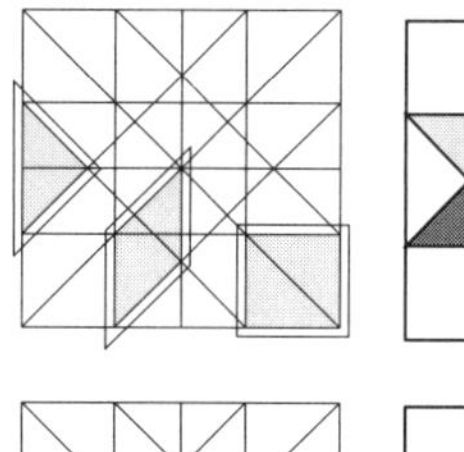
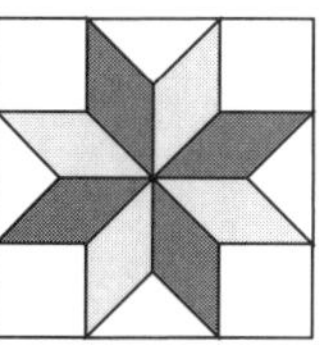
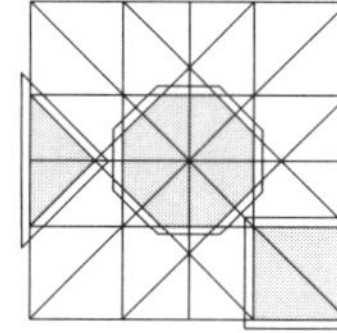

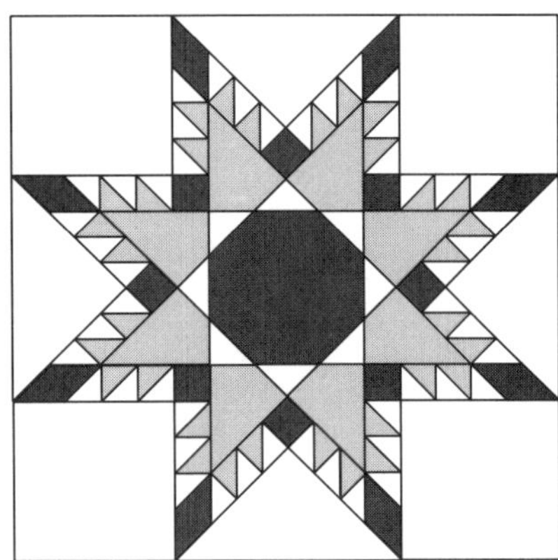

Radiant Star

The Radiant Star is probably the easiest of the Feathered Stars to draft and to piece. Most of the blocks in this book are based on slight variations of this drafting. The star features only one feather triangle size, has true diamonds at the tips, and a center octagon.

Now, usually when one drafts a patchwork design, the outside of the square is drawn first and other lines are added on the inside to make the pattern. It is difficult, though not impossible to draft a Feathered Star with that approach. I have found it easy, though, to draft Feathered Stars starting from the inside and working out. No matter what the design variation, I start with the finished size of the smallest Feather triangles and draft the block accordingly. I rarely know how large the block will be until it is drawn. In most cases, the size of the block is not important anyway; the quilt is simply designed around it.

The size of the finished block can be changed by changing the size of the feathers (e.g., from 1" to $1\frac{1}{4}$") or by changing the number of feathers (from 3 to 4 or 5) on a side.

Sometimes a specific block size is needed. Once a block is drafted in one size, it only takes a bit of simple algebra to change the finished size to another dimension. The equation explained in the next paragraph is based on a ratio or proportion. Each Feathered Star design has its own specific ratio of the size of the feather (the smallest dimension) to the size of the finished block (the largest dimension). Size changes can be made using these numbers.

Example: The 15" Radiant Star pattern given on page 22 is drafted on a 1" scale, which means the smallest triangles or feathers measure 1" finished on the short side. The finished block measures 15". When you compare the two dimensions (feather to finished block), it is called a ratio and can be expressed as a fraction $\frac{1}{15}$, which is read 1 is to 15. What if you want to make this same block in a 12" size? The question now is the size of feather that will result in a 12" finished block. Let x represent the feather dimension in the 12" block. Write the equation like this:

$\frac{1}{15} = \frac{x}{12}$ (1 is to 15 as x is 12)

Which is solved like this:

$15x = 12$

$x = \frac{12}{15}$

$x = \frac{4}{5}$

The feathers in the 12" version of the design must measure $\frac{4}{5}$". Draw the star again starting with $\frac{4}{5}$" triangles rather than 1" triangles. For this kind of dimension, use 5-squares-to-the-inch or 10-squares-to-the-inch graph paper.

Draft the 15" Radiant Star on a large sheet of $\frac{1}{8}$" graph paper. We don't have to draw the whole star, just enough of it to get one of each shape that will need to be cut. The size of the two-triangle "feather" square will be 1" finished. Study the block. Along the side of the kite shape that is the leg of the star, you'll see three 1" feather squares, so the long side of the side of the kite must measure 3". Imagine this 3" line is one side of a 45° diamond. Because all the sides of a diamond are equal, all the sides will be 3" long. Double these to 6" and you have the diagonal dimension of the first center square we will draw.

1. On the heavy lines of the graph paper, draw two 6" lines that bisect each other. Connect the end of the lines to form a square.

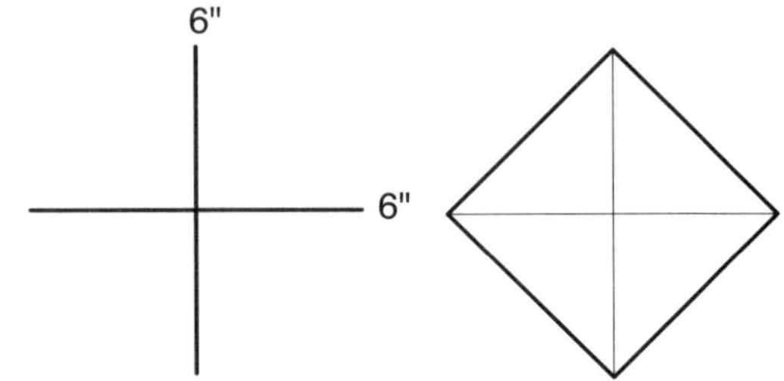

2. With your compass set at 3" (from the center of the square to one corner), draw a circle that encloses the square. The circle should pass through all the corners of the square.
3. Draw two more 6" lines that begin and end on the circle and pass through the center of the square at exactly a 45° angle. Establish the 45° angle by making sure the line you draw passes exactly corner to corner across the little squares of the graph paper. Connect the ends of these lines to form a second square. Two templates can now be identified, the center octagon (#1) and the small triangle (#2) next to it. Because of all the lines in this drawing, it is easiest to find the shapes if they are lightly shaded with colored pencils.

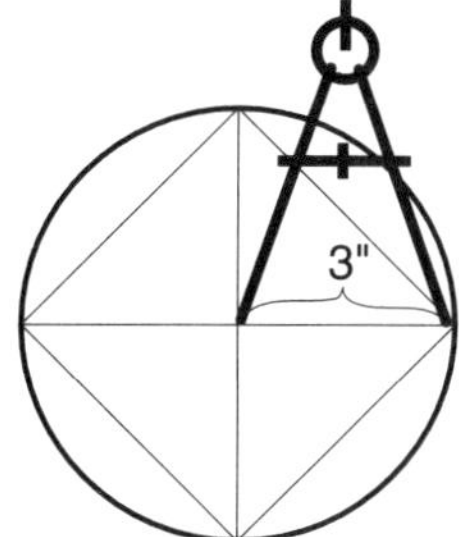

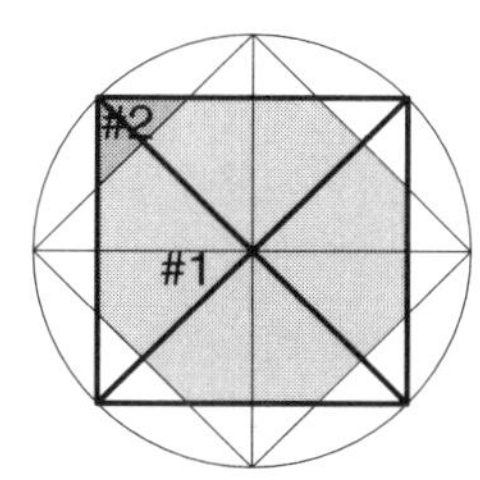

4. Extend the sides of both center squares. Let the lines cross. Now you can find Template #3, the kite shape. Check to make sure each long side of the kite measures exactly 3".

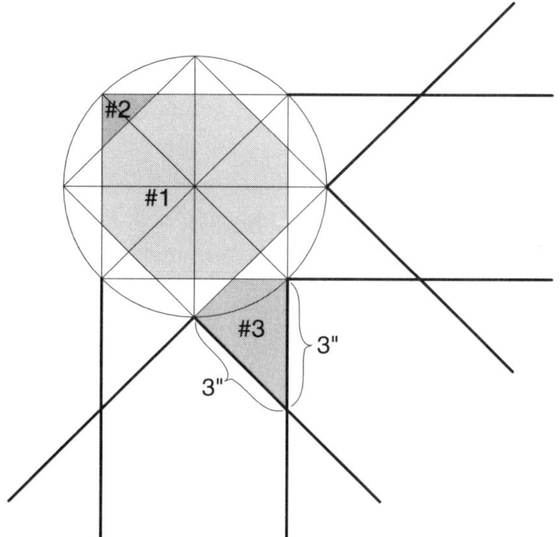

5. In what will be the lower right area of the block, draw two lines that are 1" from and parallel to the extended lines. Where the two lines cross, a 1" square, Template #4, will be formed. Draw two more 1" squares along the side of each kite. Divide each square in half to make triangles. The extra triangle at the end of the feather row will be designated as Template #5.

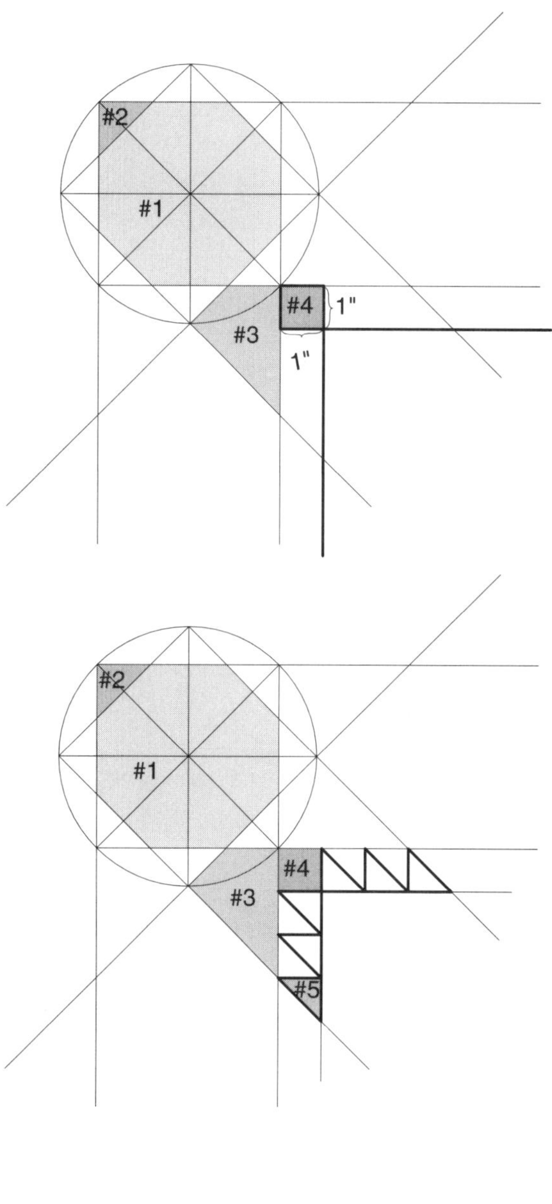

6. To make the diamond at the tip of the kite, you will need a compass. The length of the side of the diamond is equal to the long side of the #5 triangle. Following the illustration, take a compass setting of AB. From the top point of the triangle, swing the compass and strike an arc on line m creating point C. AB = AC. Without changing the compass setting, move the compass point to point B and strike an arc on line p, creating point D. Connect point C to point D. The figure just drawn is a 45° diamond with all sides equal, Template #6.

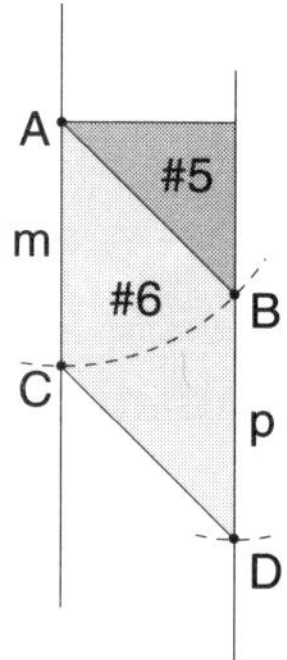

7. One side of the corner square (measure from #4 to the tip of #6) is very close to 4⅜". Using the 4⅜" dimension for each side, draw the corner square. This is Template #7.
8. The large side triangle (Template #8) is equal to half of the corner square, #7. To make that shape, simply divide the corner square in half on the diagonal.

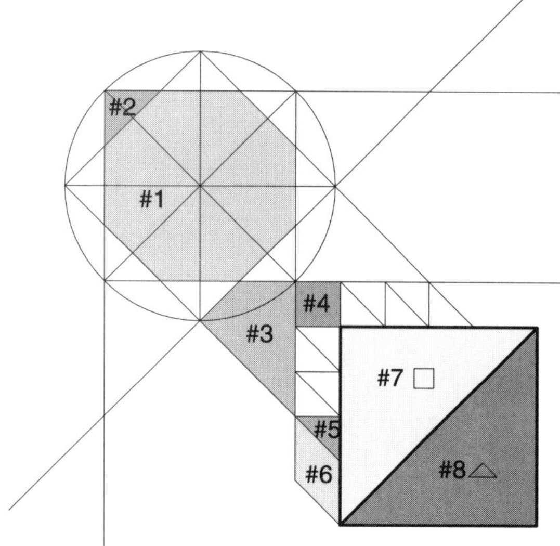

9. Add ¼" seam allowances to each identified shape to get cutting dimensions or make templates.

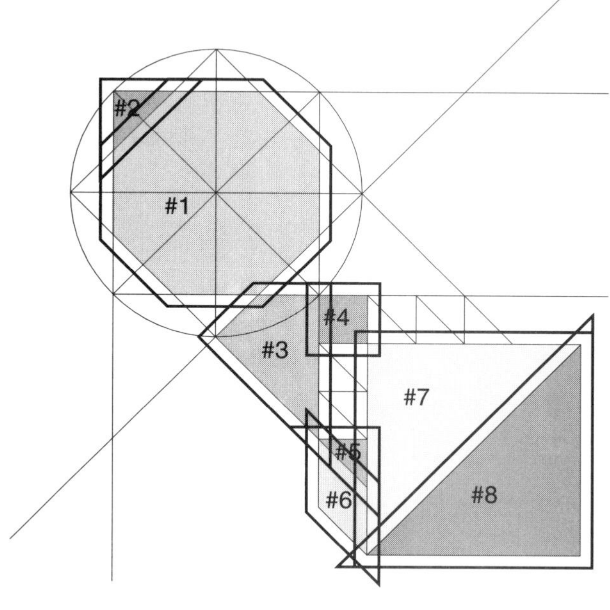

Drafting Variation

This Feathered Star with a Sunflower Center has 4 Feather Triangles instead of 3, and a circular center motif. To draft it with 1" finished Feather Squares, repeat the Radiant Star drafting replacing the 6" lines with 8" lines and use the circular guideline as a design element.

DESIGNING YOUR FEATHERED STAR QUILT

You have probably noticed that there are only block patterns included in this book, and no patterns for entire quilts. This is because most quilters who would tackle a Feathered Star also know how to design a quilt. Here are a few suggestions to help you through the process.

Feathered Stars can be very geometric and formal. To soften the look, consider using soft contrast large-scale floral prints as shown in the Golden Splendor quilt on page 27. If you are so inclined, adding appliqué elements to the blocks and borders lends a nice counterpoint to the sawtooth edges of the stars.

You can use any kind of setting arrangement with Feathered Star blocks that you can use with any other repeated block design. You can set the blocks straight or on point, next to each other, or separated by sashing or alternate blocks. Often, setting pieces to go with large blocks are also large and need to be broken up with piecing or appliqué. I like to repeat the small feather triangles in setting and border designs. Sawtooth, Delectable Mountains, and Streak of Lightning borders are traditional favorites. The largest of the Feathered Stars make great center blocks for medallion-style quilts. A good book to look at for border ideas is *Pieced Borders: The Complete Resource* by Judy Martin and Marsha McCloskey from Crosley-Griffith Publishing.

Most of the Feathered Star blocks are fairly large, so not many are needed to make a bed quilt. Many antique Feathered Star quilts were made with half-blocks along the top edge so the quilts wouldn't be too long.

If you want to set the blocks next to each other, consider eliminating the seams between the blocks to make room for uninterrupted quilting or appliqué designs. If you do this with most of the blocks in this book, you'll be adding a lot more partial seams to the construction process, but it's well worthwhile. The one block that is easy to construct this way, and doesn't involve convoluted partial piecing, is Kay's Star on page 40.

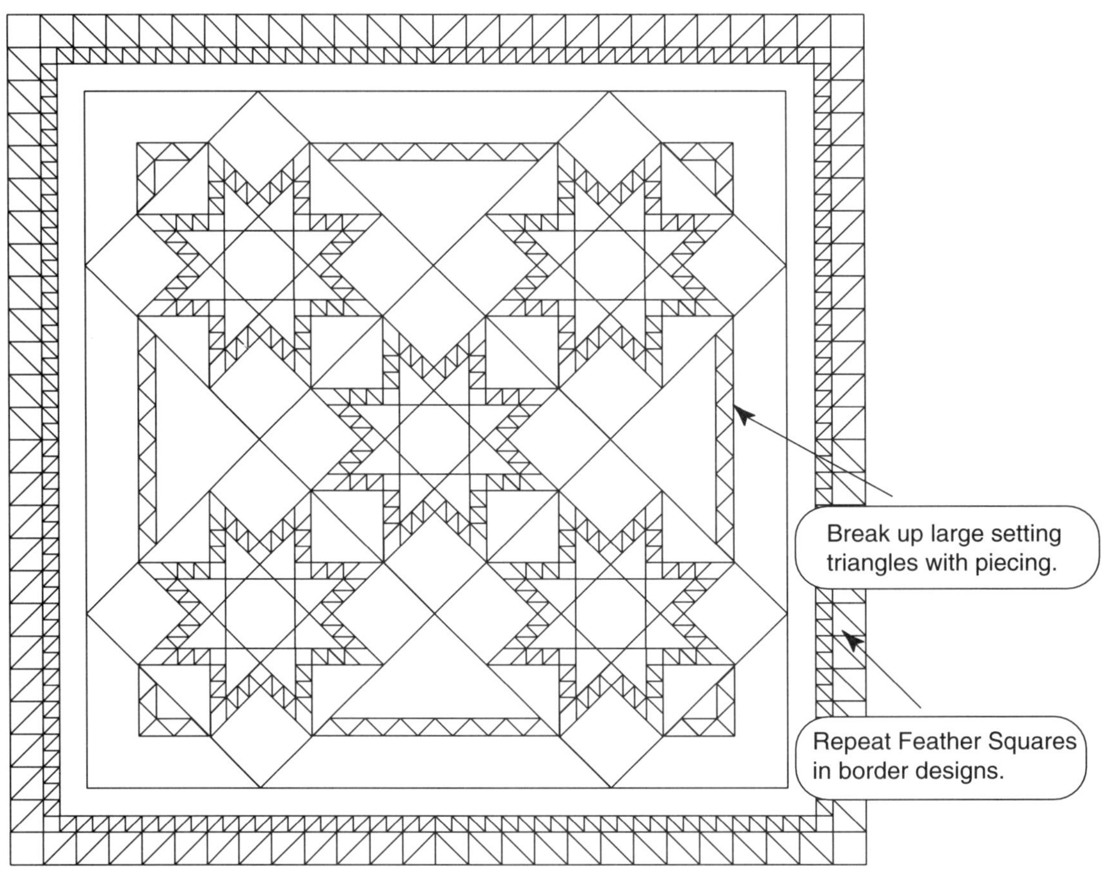
Break up large setting triangles with piecing.
Repeat Feather Squares in border designs.

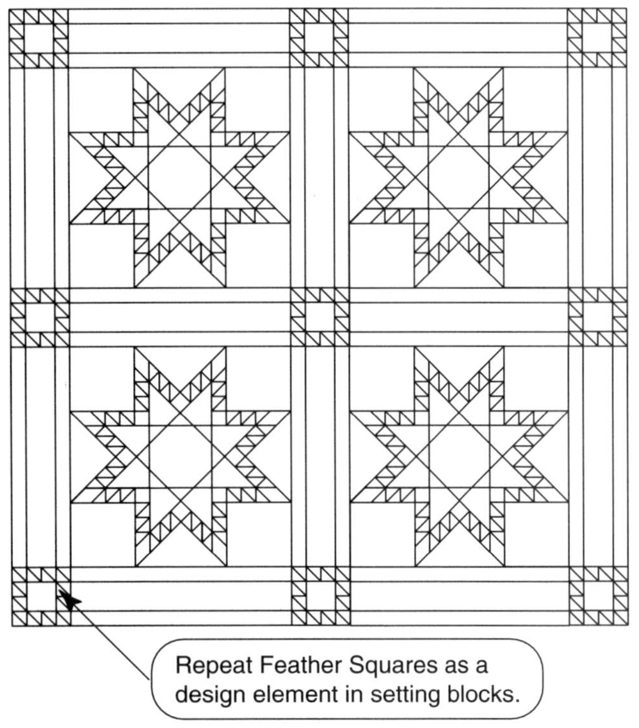
Repeat Feather Squares as a design element in setting blocks.

Use a Feathered Star block for the center of a medallion quilt or wallhanging.

Cutting the Pieces

A Word About Dimensions

If you use templates to cut patches, you will find them beginning on page 48. Look on the Cutting Chart for each star to find the template number. For rotary cutting, cut the patches according to the dimensions given and compare cut shapes to the templates to check for accuracy.

Because of the specific drafting requirements of Feathered Star blocks, cutting dimensions of individual patches are in various fractions. I have elected to round odd-ball dimensions to the nearest sixteenth of an inch. Markings on most standard cutting rulers only measure eighths. One half of an eighth is a sixteenth. The numbers in the charts for cutting sixteenths are written to the nearest eighth with a plus mark after them, e.g. 1⅞+" actually means 1¹⁵⁄₁₆". Measure the number given ***plus*** half of the next eighth. I find it helps to lay my cutting ruler directly on top of the template in the book to see how the lines on the ruler relate to the shape I want to cut. You may feel more comfortable making accurate paper or plastic templates to attach to the underside of your cutting ruler to make proper guides for cutting these sizes.

Rotary cutting dimensions given in the Cutting Charts include the ¼" seam allowance.

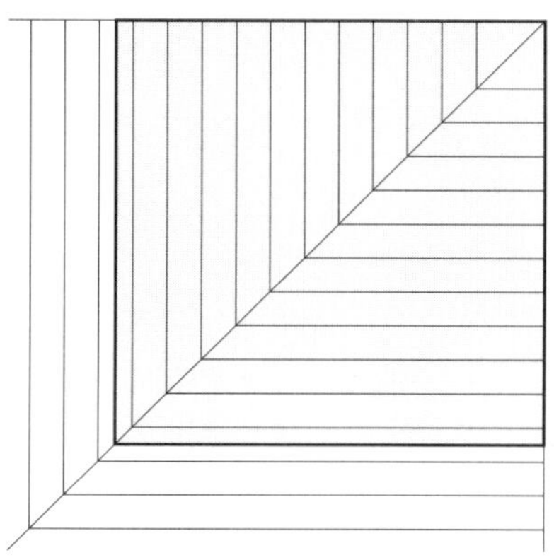

1/16" falls halfway between the 1/8" marks on a rotary cutting ruler.

Rotary Cutting

Tools

For rotary cutting the patches, you will need a rotary cutter with a fresh blade, a cutting mat, and various cutting rulers. Rulers for rotary cutting are ⅛" thick transparent acrylic and come in an array of sizes with a variety of markings. The rulers most frequently used are :

- 6" x 24" Omnigrid™ marked in 1", ¼" and ⅛" increments
- 8" Bias Square™ ruler (a square ruler marked in ⅛" increments with a 45° angle line running corner to corner) used for bias-strip piecing two-triangle Feather Squares (see page 12). This ruler also comes as a 4" or 6" square. You may find these smaller rulers easier to use for cutting the very small Feather Squares in the Double and Triple Feathered Stars.
- 15" square ruler for cutting the large beginning square for bias-strip piecing
- Precision Trimmer 3™ for marking ¼" stitching points on set-in seams and for trimming points for easy matching

Straight Strips

The rotary method of cutting many shapes begins with cutting strips of fabric. I prefer to cut strips on lengthwise grain, parallel to the selvage. Fold the fabric so cuts will be parallel to the selvage. Trim away selvage and make successive cuts measuring from the first cut. All strips are cut with the ¼" seam allowance included. This method works especially well when working with fat quarters.

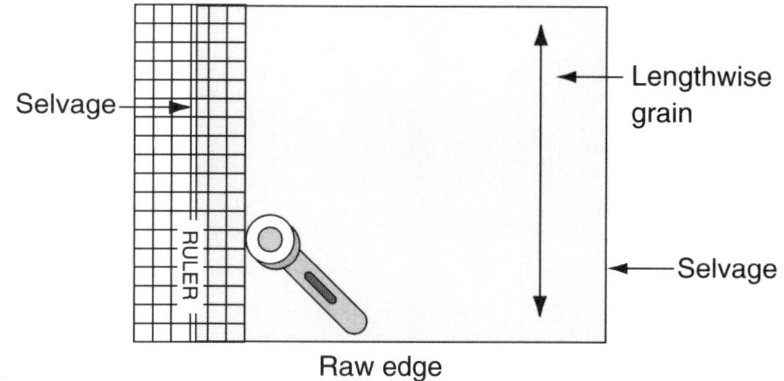

Squares and Rectangles

To cut squares, first cut fabric in strips using the measurement listed in the Cutting Chart. Cut across the strips at the same interval to make squares.

Cut rectangles in the same manner, first cutting strips the width of the rectangle then cutting to the proper length.

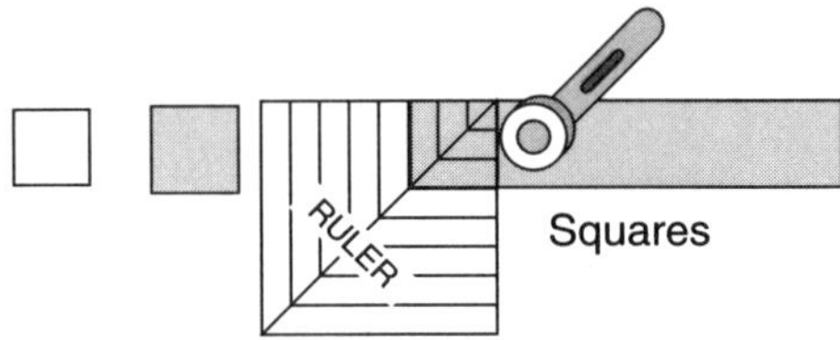

Trapezoids

The instructions given for cutting Trapezoids for the Double and Triple Feathered Star blocks have you cut rectangles and then make a 45° angle cut at one end. The trapezoids for Kay's Star are cut from half- and quarter-square triangles. Templates are given for these shapes with special cutting instructions.

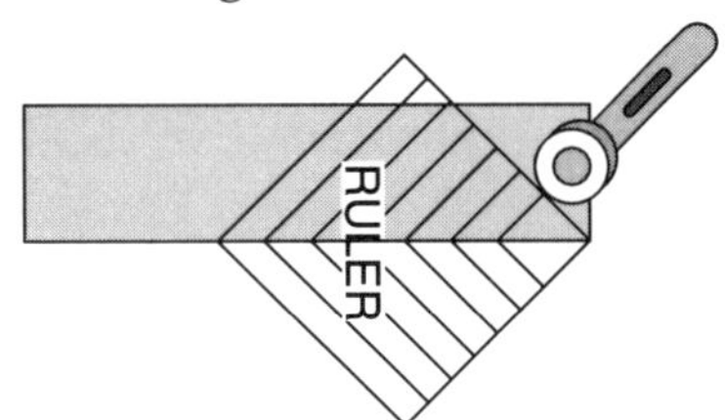

Half-Square Triangles

In the Cutting Charts, half-square triangles are indicated first by a triangle sitting on its short side and second by a square with a diagonal line through it.

To cut them, cut a square and then cut it in half diagonally once. The resulting two triangles will have short sides on the straight grain of the fabric and the long side on the bias. Trim points for matching according to the template given.

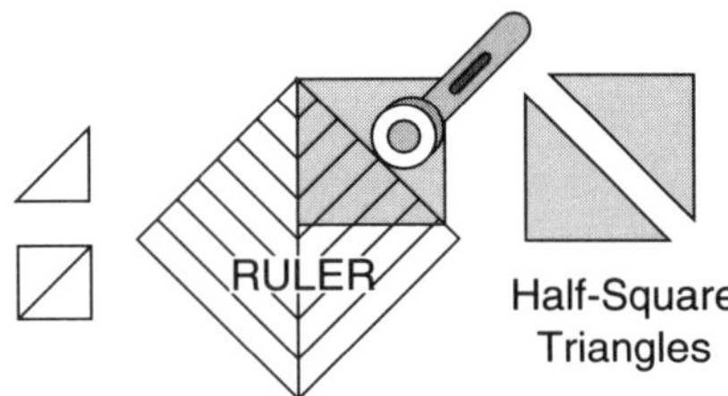

Quarter-Square Triangles

In the Cutting Charts, quarter-square triangles are indicated first by a triangle sitting on its long side and second by a square with an X in it.

To cut these triangles, cut a square then cut it in half diagonally twice. The resulting four triangles will have the long side on the straight grain and the short sides on the bias. Trim points for matching according to the template given

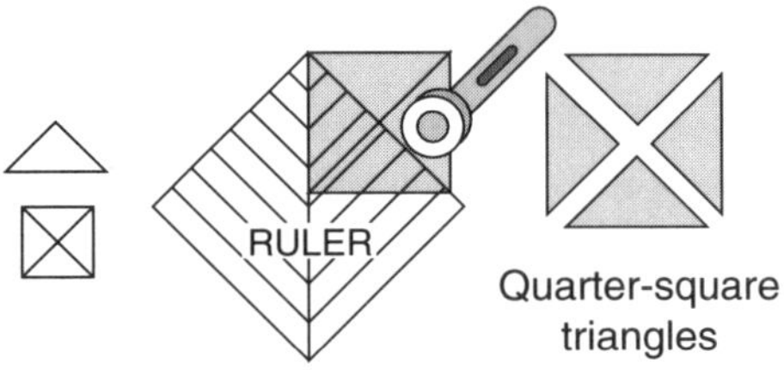

Kites

For want of a better word, I call template #K4 in the Radiant Star pattern on page 22, a "kite" (when I was a kid, kites were shaped like this and were made of wood, paper and string ....) To cut a kite shape:

1. Cut a square to the dimensions given in the Cutting Chart and cut it in half to make half-square triangles. Carefully stack the triangles so they can be trimmed at the same time.
2. On the long side of the triangle, measure from the triangle point the distance equal to the side of the square that was cut in step one. Cut off the triangular section that sticks out. This will yield a kite shape with two long sides equal and two short sides equal.

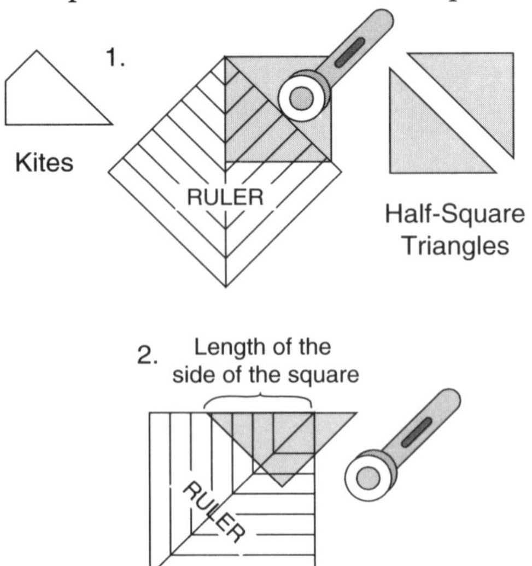

Octagons

To cut an Octagon, first cut a square to the dimensions given in the Cutting Chart, then trim each corner using a triangular paper or plastic Cutaway template attached to the underside of a cutting ruler for a guide. Cutaway templates in the proper dimensions are given with the Octagon templates on page 50-51. Though you can make them with paper and attach them to your ruler with tape; I use a product called Static Stickers™, a pink-colored plastic film that sticks to plastic rulers by static. It can be repositioned and leaves no sticky residue.

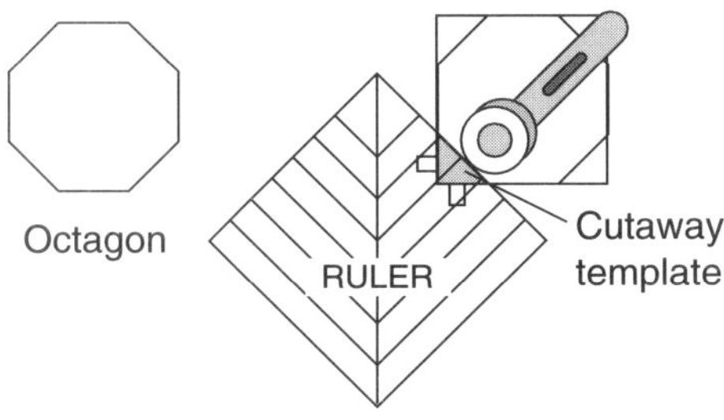

Diamonds

Cut a strip of fabric the width of the dimension given in the Cutting Chart. Make a 45° angle cut at one end of the strip. Make additional successive cuts parallel to the 45° angle cut using the same dimension as the width of the strip. Check the 45° angle from time to time as you are making these cuts.

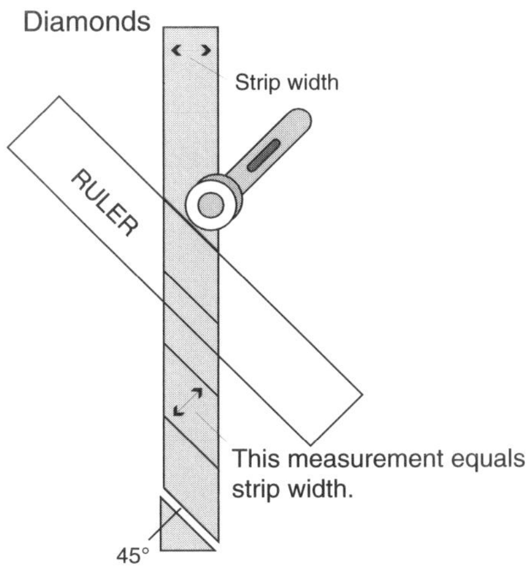

Trimming Points for Easy Matching

Trimming points from triangles and other shapes takes the guesswork out of matching cut patches before sewing them together. Once you've trimmed the points, patches will fit flush with one another when correctly aligned. This is especially important in Feathered Stars for a number of reasons.

First, trimming points eliminates bulk in seams and prevents show-through of dark fabrics. Most quilters trim points after sewing anyway, so why not trim them before the seams are sewn? Second, untrimmed points tend to drag through the sewing machine preventing accurate piecing — especially on tiny patches. Last, trimming points allows you to easily match one patch to another, eliminating the guessing, pinning and matching of patch centers.

Templates in this book have trimming lines indicated. Points have been left on to make measuring for rotary cutting easier. When trimming triangle points, it's important to remember that points can be trimmed in two different ways: perpendicular to the short sides, or perpendicular to the long side. The direction of the trim lines depends on how the triangle is to be sewn to the next shape, but the amount you trim will always be ⅜" on 45° angles. The illustrations here show two ways to trim triangles using the Precision Trimmer 3.

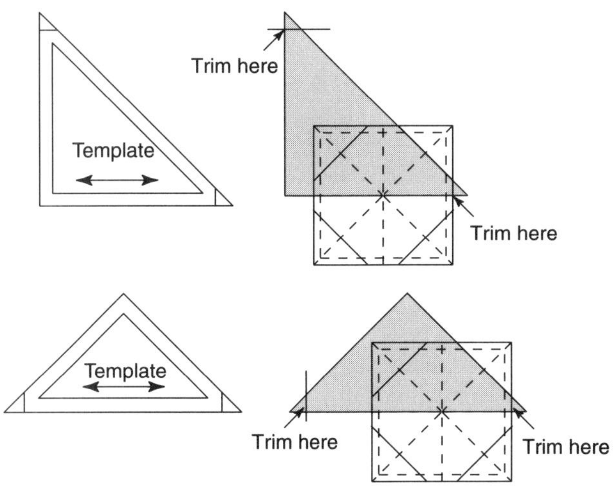

MAKING FEATHER TRIANGLES WITH BIAS-STRIP PIECING

I use Bias-Strip Piecing to make the smallest triangle units or Feather Squares in the Feathered Star blocks. Each Feather Square is made of two triangles but is actually cut as a square. In this method, large beginning squares of fabric are cut into bias strips, which are then sewn together. Squares are then each cut with the seam line centered corner to corner. Because seams are initially sewn on bias edges, the cut squares have the straight grain on the outer edges. The yield chart on page 13 shows the number of Feather Squares that can be cut from different sizes of beginning squares. The example shown in the steps below is for 12" beginning squares which will usually yield enough Feather Squares for one 12"-15" Feathered Star block.

To avoid struggling with a lot of yardage, begin by cutting the fabric that will be cut into bias strips into manageable pieces. Squares that measure 8" to 15" and fit nicely on the cutting mat are preferable.

1. Cut two 12"-beginning squares of contrasting fabrics. Layer fabrics with right sides facing and cut both squares at the same time using a large square ruler. Edges of these squares should line up with straight grain.
2. Make a diagonal cut corner to corner across the squares to establish the true bias (45° angle).

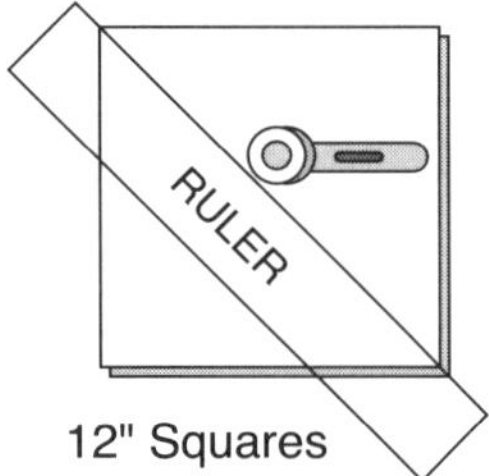

12" Squares

3. Measuring from the center cut, cut strips 2" wide. Continue until the whole square has been cut into bias strips. There will be six sets of strips (2 long, 2 medium and 2 short) plus corner triangles. The number of strips will vary depending on the size of the beginning squares.

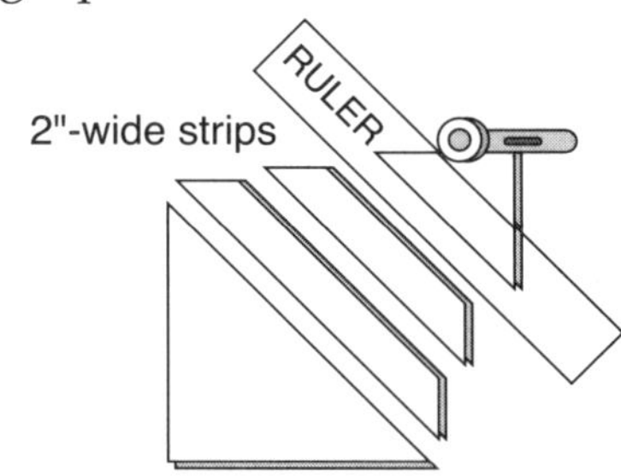

4. Pick up pairs of contrasting strips; they will be right sides together and ready to stitch. Sew them together on the long bias edge, using a ¼" seam allowance. Press seams open.

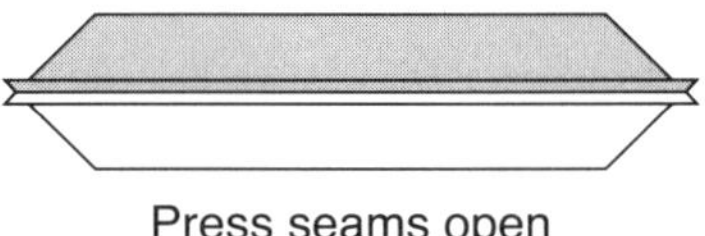

Press seams open

5. Sew strip pairs together as shown. There will be strip pairs of varying lengths. The most efficient configuration for sewing them together is shown here. Sew the longest strip pairs together, then the next longest, etc. Keep the "Vs" along the bottom edge even. Corner triangles left over after cutting strips can also be sewn together. Press seams open.

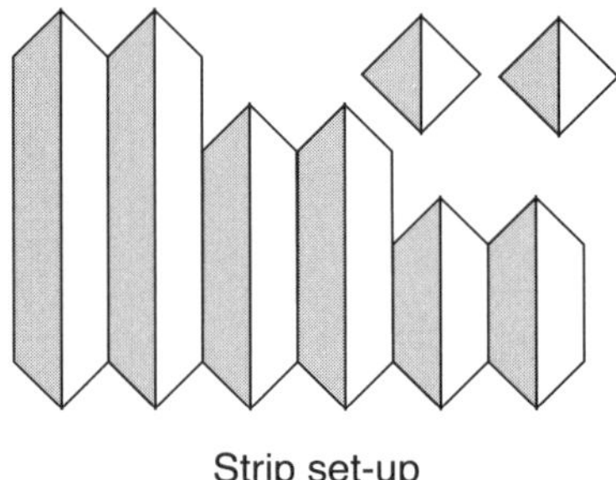

Strip set-up

6. The Cutting Charts with each block pattern tell what size to cut the Feather Squares. Using a square cutting ruler (my favorite is the Bias Square™ from Martingale) and rotary

cutter, begin cutting the first row of Feather Squares at the lowest points as shown. Place the diagonal line of the ruler on the first seam line. Cut squares slightly (a few threads to ⅛") larger than the desired cut size of the Feather Square. Two cuts are required to separate the square from the sewn strips. Let your rotary cutter go a few threads beyond the seam line on each cut to cleanly separate the square without leaving a maddening two threads uncut. If you have joined two or more sets of strips, cut squares from alternate seam lines working across the strips from one side to the other. After cutting the first set of squares, go back and cut from the skipped seam lines. The squares cut from the strips now must be cut to the exact size desired. Turn each square so the two sides that were just cut are pointing towards you. Align the diagonal line of the square rotary cutting ruler with the seam line of the square and the exact dimension on the ruler with the cut sides of the square. Make the final two cuts.

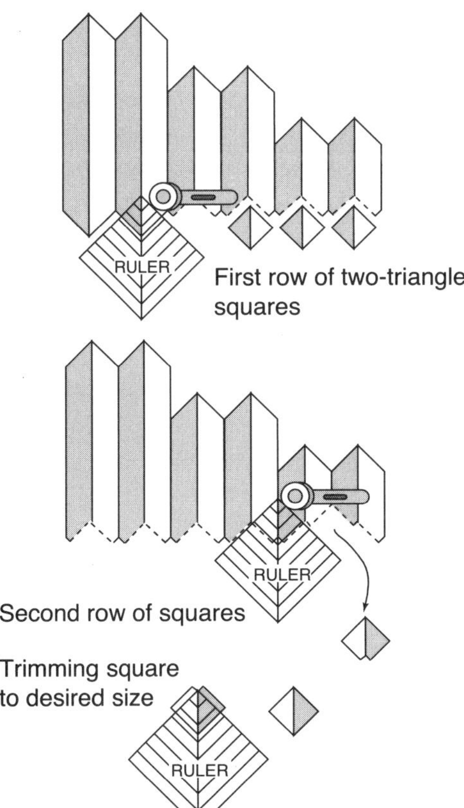

Yield Chart

This chart tells the number of 1½" (cut size) Feather Squares that can be cut from various sizes of beginning squares. Large beginning squares will obviously yield more feathers than smaller ones. Individual sewing and cutting habits will affect the yield. I use a strip width of 2" when cutting feathers because it is an easy number to remember and cut. The width is a little wide for the 1½" square size, but it will also accommodate feathers cut in slightly larger sizes. If your feathers are to be cut smaller than 1½", the bias strips could be cut narrower, but I find it difficult to press seams open when strips are less than 2" wide. If the cutting dimension of the Feather Square is larger than 2", a wider strip should be used.

Yield Chart for Feather Squares			
One light and one dark Beginning Square 2"-wide bias strips/corner triangles used			
Beginning Square Size	No. of Strip Sets	Cut Size	Yield
6"	2	1-1/2" x 1-1/2"	10
8"	4	1-1/2" x 1-1/2"	21
10"	4	1-1/2" x 1-1/2"	35
12"	6	1-1/2" x 1-1/2"	50
13 1/2"	6	1-1/2" x 1-1/2"	61
15"	8	1-1/2" x 1-1/2"	84

Formula for Strip Width

To figure the proper strip width for bias-strip piecing other sizes of Feather Squares, do this:

1. On graph paper, draw a square the finished size of the Feather Square. Add a ¼" seam allowance. Draw a diagonal line across the whole square.
2. Measure from the center diagonal line to one corner of the square. This distance is "x".
3. To get the proper strip width, add ¾" for seam allowances and "wiggle room." If the number doesn't match the lines on your cutting ruler or will be hard to cut, round the number up to one that will be easy to measure.

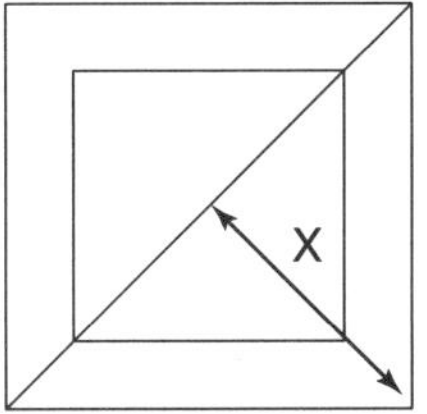

X + 3/4"= strip width for bias-strip piecing

General Piecing

Feathered Stars can be pieced entirely on the sewing machine. But, there are a lot of seams and it is important to be as accurate as possible. This is a design that demands all your piecing skills.

Presser Foot

My favorite machine-piecing presser foot is the straight-stitching foot for my old Singer Featherweight. The #13 foot for the Bernina has the same configuration. It is an open-toed foot with the right side narrower than the left. The narrower inner "toe" lets me see the edge of the fabric as it is being sewn. The absence of any bar in front of the needle, lets me see the needle as it enters the fabric.

Needle

Put a fresh needle in your machine. A "sharp" needle rather than a "universal needle" will make a better straight stitch. Also, change the face plate on the machine to one with a small round hole for straight stitching. (Be sure to change it back before zig-zagging again!)

Thread

Use 100 percent cotton white or neutral thread as light as the lightest fabric in the project. Use dark neutral thread for piecing dark solids. I choose one color of thread and use it to piece the whole quilt regardless of color changes in the fabric. Lighter threads, if they don't get trimmed completely, will not show through light fabrics in the finished quilt.

Stitch Length

Stitch length should be set at 10-12 stitches to the inch (2 – 2.5 millimeters). Stitches should be short and strong, but not so tight that the blade of a seam ripper cannot be easily slipped between the thread and the fabric to break a stitch.

Accurate ¼" Seams

Sew accurate ¼" seams and check your cutting and piecing for accuracy before you get too far along in the block. To determine the proper seam allowance on your sewing machine, I suggest you do two things. First, take a small piece of ⅛" or ¼" graph paper with one edge cut very carefully on a blue line and place it under the presser foot. Lower the needle into the ¼" seam line. The edge of the paper falls where the edge of the fabric should be when you are stitching. If there is no appropriate marking on the machine, lay a piece of blue painter's tape along the edge of the graph paper to act as the ¼" guide.

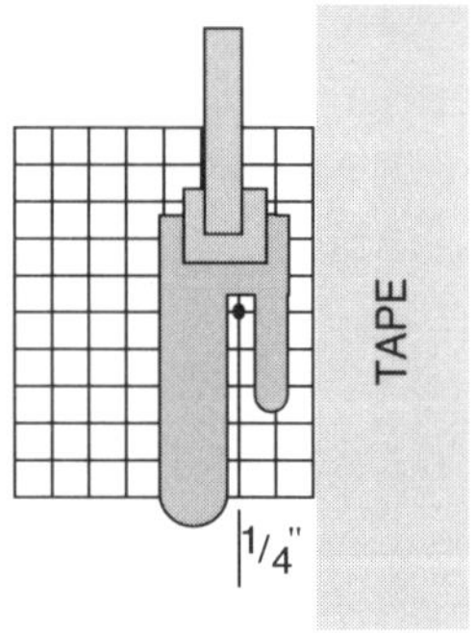

Second, test your cutting and piecing for accuracy. An easy test is to cut three 1½" Feather Squares as described on pages 12 and 13. Sew them together with your best ¼" seam allowance. Press the seams open and measure the resulting strip: it should be exactly 3½" long. If it isn't, your seams are either too deep or too shallow and will need to be adjusted before you piece your star.

Accuracy test

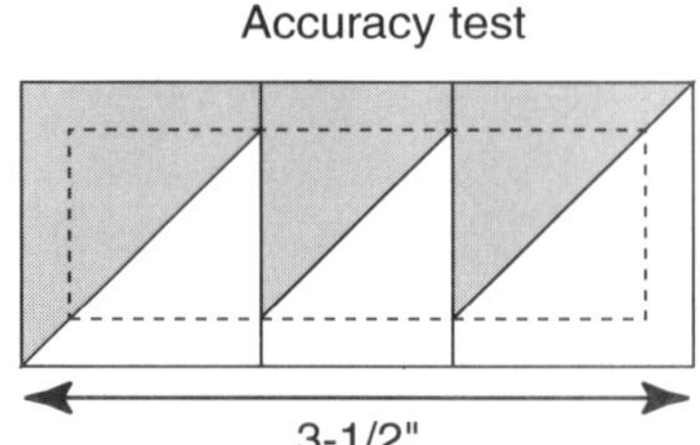

Leader Strip

Use a Leader Strip to control threads and save time and thread by chain piecing. A leader strip is a strip of fabric about 12-15 inches long and 2" wide. It can be a scrap or something you cut for this purpose. Fold the strip in half lengthwise and stitch over one end of it. Then, to chain piece, place two cut patches right sides together and without lifting the presser foot or cutting any threads, sew the seam. Your sewn patches and the leader strip will be connected by a little twist of thread. Continue sewing patches together in the same manner until you have completed as many as you want. Then, pull the Leader Strip around and stitch part way over the free end. Leaving the Leader Strip in place, and without lifting the presser foot, cut the chain-pieced units free. Snip them apart and press.

Get Organized

Organize your sewing to save time and avoid confusion. As you cut the patches separate them in resealable plastic bags and label each separate bag with the template number. When you are ready to sew, lay the cut patches out on the sewing table to make sure all the necessary patches have been cut and to check the color arrangement. Then separate the patches into the major piecing units. The side and corner units can usually be stacked "four deep" to maximize chain piecing possibilities and keep mirror image feather rows in their places. Refer often to the design drawings and piecing illustrations to keep the light and dark patches in the correct orientation. It is very easy in Feathered Stars to reverse Feather Squares. Sew the smallest pieces together first to form units. Join smaller units to form larger ones until the block is complete.

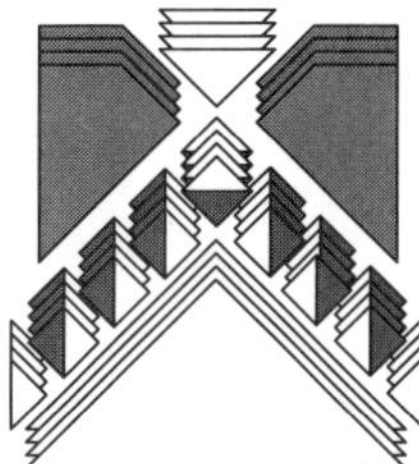

Side Units
stacked 4 deep

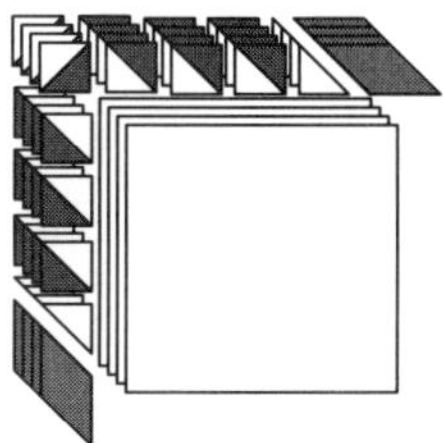

Corner Units
stacked 4 deep

Pressing

Press seams gently as the sewing progresses. Overpressing with too much heat or steam can distort fabric shapes. The instructions for Bias-Strip Piecing on pages 12-13 call for seam allowances to be pressed open. Press seams open as you stitch the feather rows as well. It distributes the bulk of the seam allowances and makes a flatter piece of work with crisply matched triangle points. When feather rows are sewn to the adjacent patches, it would be nearly impossible to continue pressing seams open: the seams now fall naturally to one side and in general, the rest of the seams should be pressed to whichever side they want to go. Plan pressing to take advantage of opposing seams when possible. Press seams that need to match in opposite directions to hold each other in place and distribute bulk.

Matching

Sew with the feather rows on top so matching points can be clearly seen. When seams are pressed open on feather rows, the wrong side of the work will look like the illustration below. Stitch right through the point indicated for crisp triangle points.

Match and pin seams with care. Trim lines on templates are provided to help match patches for stitching. Short seams need not be pinned unless matching is involved or the seam is more than 4" long. Keep pins away from the seam line when ever possible. Stitching over pins makes it difficult to be accurate in tight places and tends to burr the needle.

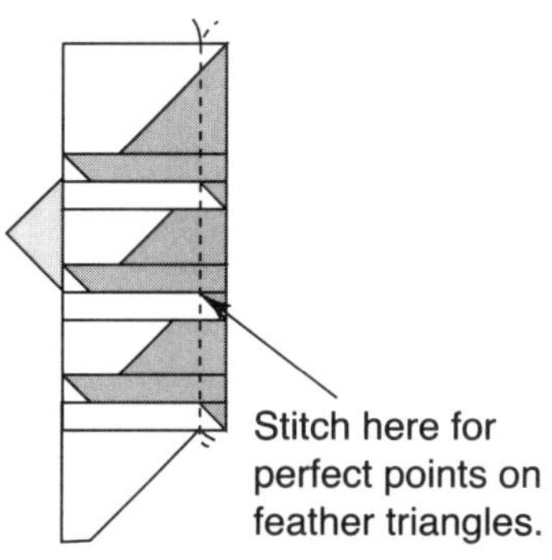

Use a positioning pin to match points at the top of the diamond on star tips. A pin carefully pushed straight through two points that need to match and pulled tight will establish the proper point of matching. Pin the seam normally and remove the positioning pin before stitching.

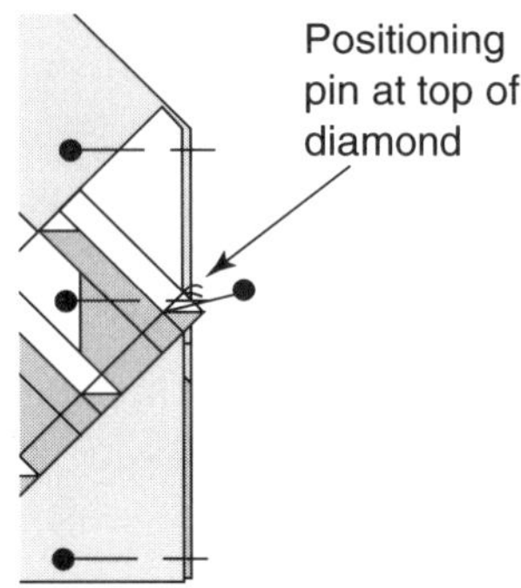

Partial Seams

Use partial seams to avoid set-in seams. Many Feathered Stars contain seams that are sewn in two parts. In the piecing illustrations, these seams are indicated by heavy lines and need to be stitched in the order given. A partial seam is one that is sewn part way early in block construction, and then completed in the last stages of sewing. Begin and end partial seams with a backtack where the stitches will not be crossed and held by another line of stitching.

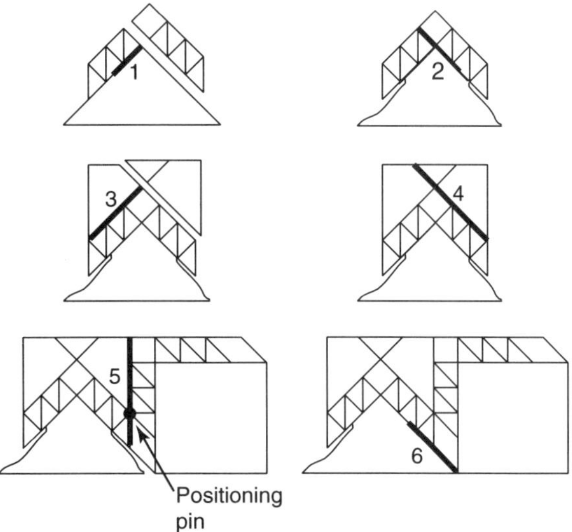

Set-in Seams

Set-in seams are needed to make the Le Moyne Stars in the center of the many of the Le Moyne-based Feathered Stars. What follows are general instructions. In the pattern directions the corner squares may be triangles instead, or be made of two triangles. The set-in seam information is important for the Feathered Le Moyne Star on page 20 and the Triple Feathered Star on page 44. In general where three seams come together in a Y, stop all stitching at the ¼" seam line and backtack. I mark these points the wrong side of the fabric. Don't let even one stitch extend beyond the marked seam allowance. As each seam is finished, take the work out of the sewing machine, position the next seam, and start stitching in the new direction. Backtacking is necessary because these seams will not be crossed and held by any other stitches.

Mark the ¼" seam allowance with the Precision Trimmer 3™.

Mark this starting and stopping point for stitching with a light fabric marker or pencil. Position the Precision Trimmer 3™ as shown, and then mark on the wrong side of the fabric, sticking the pencil point through the small hole located in one corner.

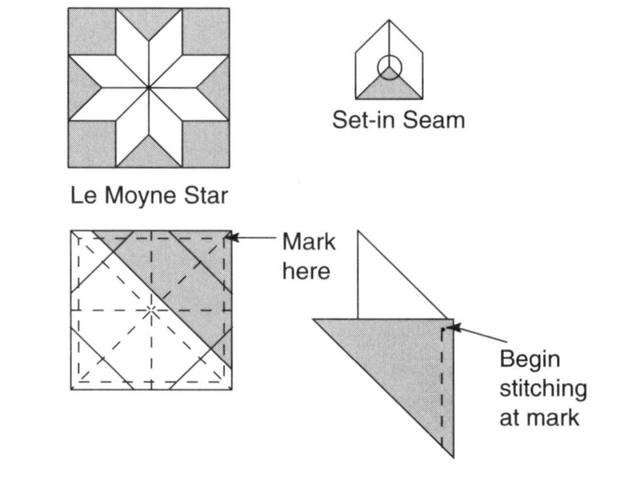

How to Piece the Le Moyne Star

1. Lay the cut pieces out to determine which to sew together first. Begin with Unit A, the diamond-diamond-triangle unit. Make four. Refer to the illustrations and follow these steps:

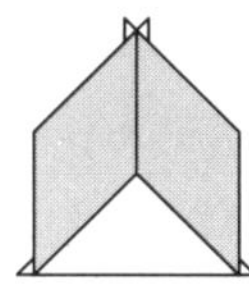

Unit A

a. Sew a diamond to a triangle. With triangle on top, begin to sew at the ¼" seam line. Mark the starting point with a long-nibbed marking pen and the Precision Trimmer 3™. Backtack by sewing two stitches forward and two stitches back, taking care not to stitch into the seam allowance. Sew the remainder of the seam, ending at the cut edge of the fabric. (No backtack is necessary here as the seam will be crossed and held by another.)

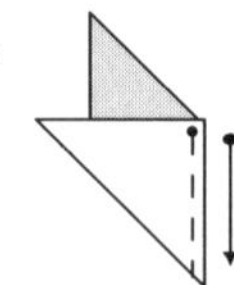

a.

b. Sew the second diamond to the same triangle. With the triangle on top, sew from the outside edge of the fabric, ending with a backtack at the ¼" seam line.

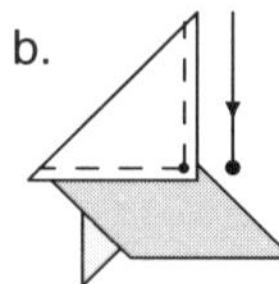

b.

c. Folding the triangle out of the way, match the points of the diamond to position them for the third seam. Stitch the diamonds together, beginning with a backtack at the inner ¼" seam line and ending at the raw edge of the fabric.

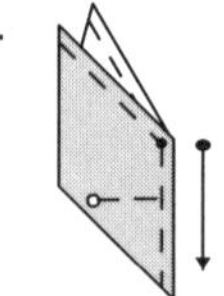

c.

d. With an iron, gently press the center seam open. Press the other two seams toward the diamonds.

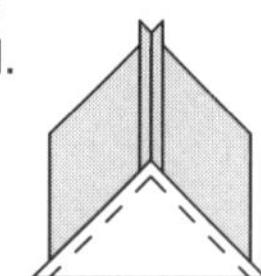

d.

2. Make four Unit B. Sew a corner square (sometimes, this is made of two triangles) to the right edge of each completed Unit A. With the square on top, begin stitching with a backtack at the inner ¼" seam line and sew to the outside raw edge.

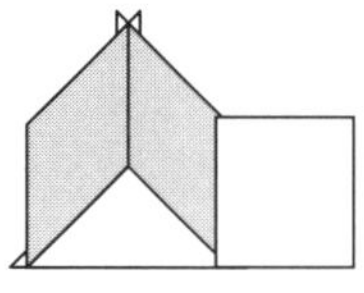

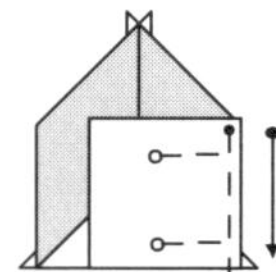

Unit B

3. Make two Units C.

a. Join two Unit Bs to form each Unit C by first matching the square of one Unit C to the diamond of the next. With the square on top, stitch from the outside edge, ending with a backtack at the inner ¼" seam line.

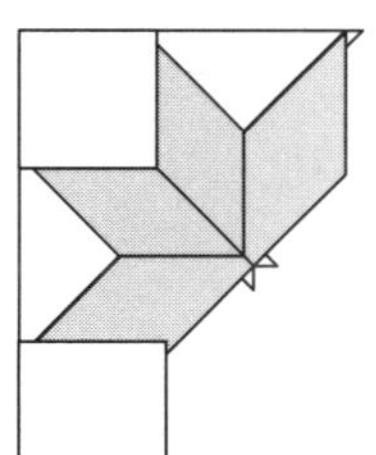

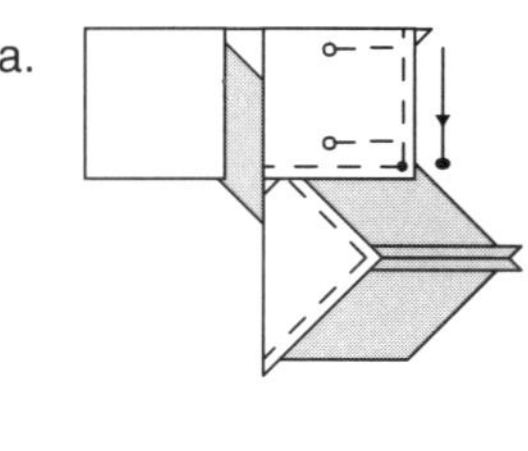

a.

b. To sew the diamonds together, match the points, folding the rest of the piecing out of the way. Use a positioning pin to match the center seams. Pin normally; remove the positioning pin. Beginning with a backtack, stitch from the inner ¼" seam line through the center seams to the raw edge of the fabric. Press center seams open and corner-square seams toward the center.

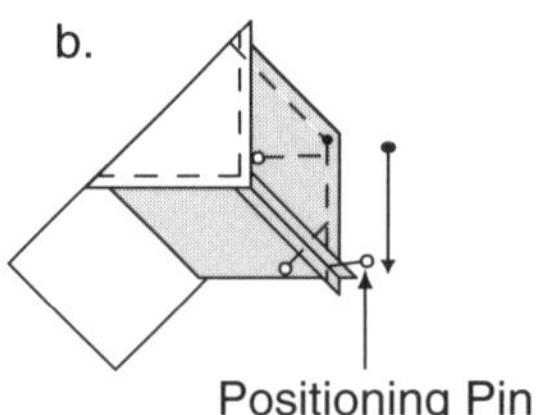

b.

4. Finish the block.

a & b. To finish the block will take three more seams. First, follow the procedure as in step 3a to join the corner squares to diamonds joining the two Unit Cs.

c. The final seam is the center seam. Use a positioning pin to carefully match the diamonds at the center point. Pin the seam securely and remove the positioning pin before stitching. Backtacking at the ¼" seam line, stitch precisely through the center, ending with another backtack at the ¼" seam.

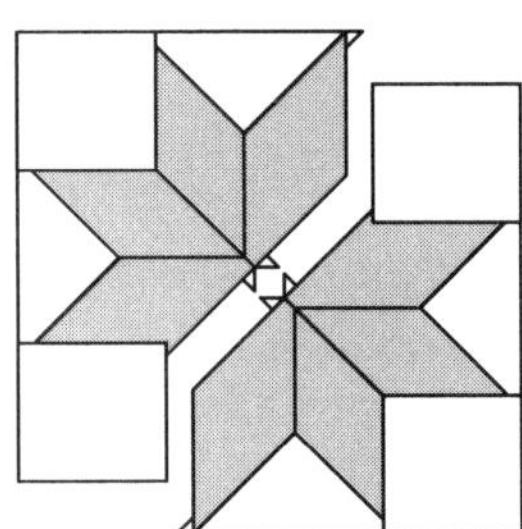

Two Unit Cs

a.

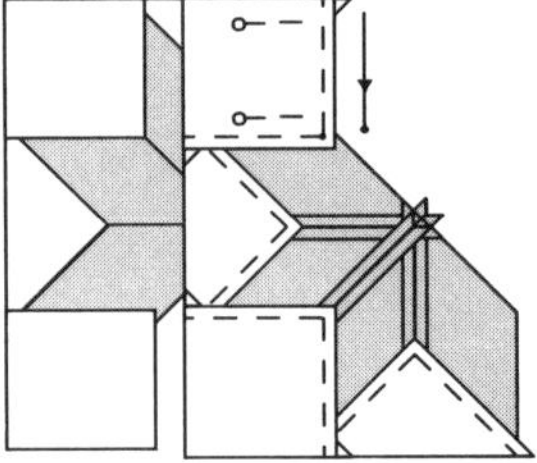

b.

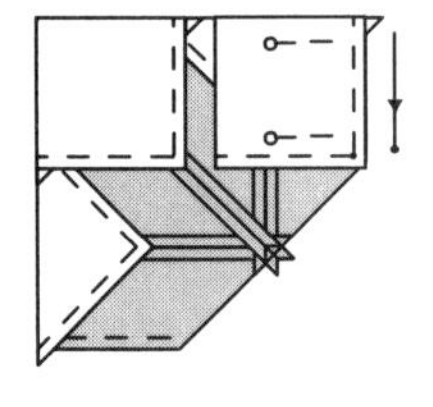

c.

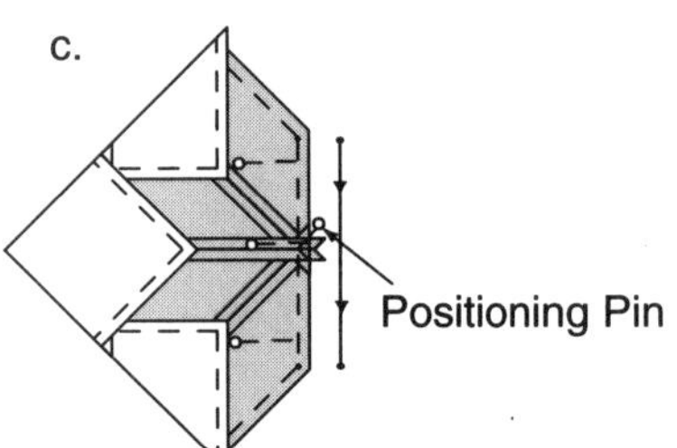

d. Press the center seam open and the remaining seams toward the center.

d.

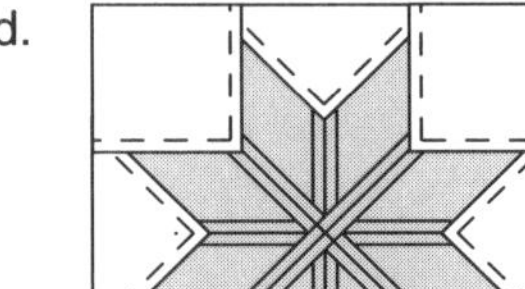

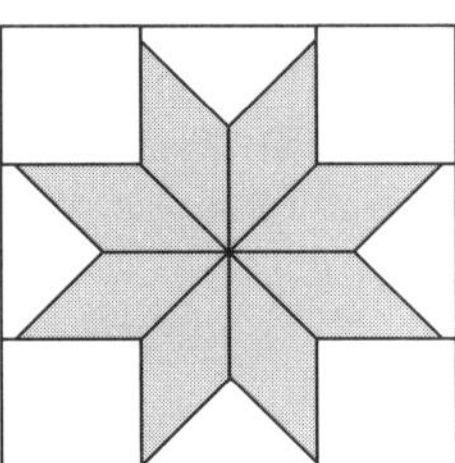

Pressing

FEATHERED STAR QUILT BLOCK PATTERNS

The block patterns begin on the next page. There are 10 different Feathered Star blocks. All the blocks have a traditional look, but some are original designs made especially for this book. Some are given in two or three different sizes. Most offer multiple shading and design ideas. The patterns support both rotary cutting and template based techniques.

Shaded Drawing
This drawing is the version of the block given in the Cutting Chart. If you choose a different arrangement of values, you will need to adjust the cutting accordingly. Refer to the photos in the Gallery for more color and fabric ideas.

Piecing Instructions
This part shows how to sew the pieces together. Refer to General Piecing on page 14 for more explanation of special techniques used in making the blocks. Many designs include partial seams that are indicated by heavy lines and labeled with numbers that show sewing order.

Line Drawing
This drawing can be photocopied and enlarged if you want to experiment with various colorations. The different shapes are designated by template name and refer to the Cutting Chart. Templates can be found beginning on page 48.

Bias-Strip Piecing
This information is about making the small Feather triangles with the bias-strip piecing method described on page 12. Here, you'll find: beginning square dimensions, strip width, and number and cutting size of Feather Squares.

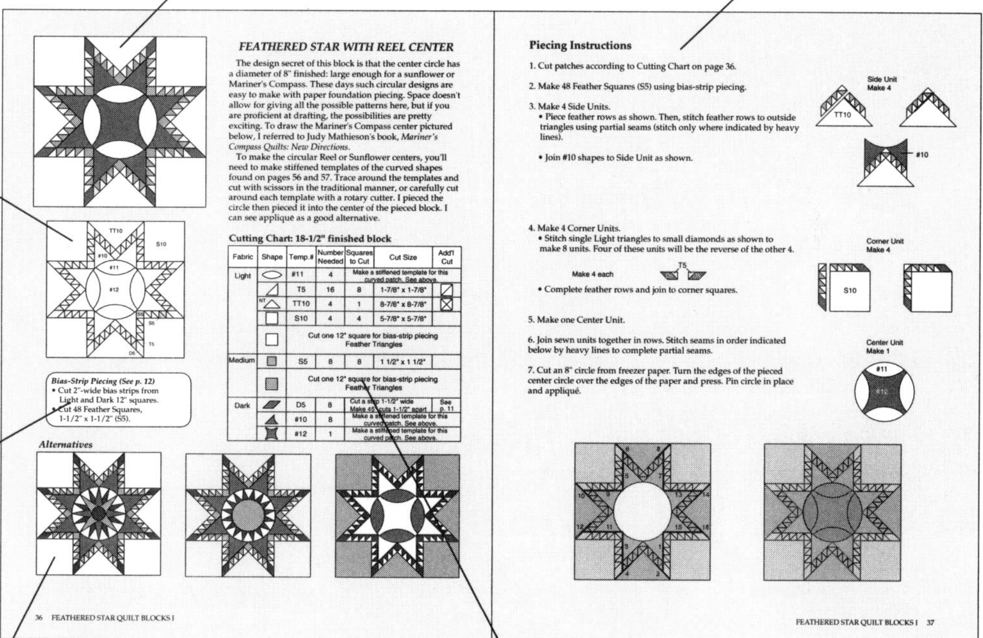

FEATHERED STAR WITH REEL CENTER

The design secret of this block is that the center circle has a diameter of 8" finished: large enough for a sunflower or Mariner's Compass. These days such circular designs are easy to make with paper foundation piecing. Space doesn't allow for giving all the possible patterns here, but if you are proficient at drafting, the possibilities are pretty exciting. To draw the Mariner's Compass center pictured below, I referred to Judy Mathieson's book, *Mariner's Compass Quilts: New Directions*.

To make the circular Reel or Sunflower centers, you'll need to make stiffened templates of the curved shapes found on pages 56 and 57. Trace around the templates and cut with scissors in the traditional manner, or carefully cut around each template with a rotary cutter. I pieced the circle then pieced it into the center of the pieced block. I can see appliqué as a good alternative.

Cutting Chart: 18-1/2" finished block

Fabric	Shape	Temp.#	Number Needed	Squares to Cut	Cut Size	Add'l Cut
Light		#11	4	Make a stiffened template for this curved patch. See above.		
		T5	16	8	1-7/8" x 1-7/8"	
	NT	TT10	4	1	8-7/8" x 8-7/8"	
		S10	4	4	5-7/8" x 5-7/8"	
		Cut one 12" square for bias-strip piecing Feather Triangles				
Medium		S5	8	8	1 1/2" x 1 1/2"	
		Cut one 12" square for bias-strip piecing Feather Triangles				
Dark		D5	8	Cut a strip 1-1/2" wide Make 45° cuts 1-1/2" apart		See p. 11
		#10	8	Make a stiffened template for this curved patch. See above.		
		#12	1	Make a stiffened template for this curved patch. See above.		

Bias-Strip Piecing (See p. 12)
- Cut 2"-wide bias strips from Light and Dark 12" squares.
- Cut 48 Feather Squares, 1-1/2" x 1-1/2" (S5).

Alternatives

36 FEATHERED STAR QUILT BLOCKS I

Piecing Instructions

1. Cut patches according to Cutting Chart on page 36.
2. Make 48 Feather Squares (S5) using bias-strip piecing.
3. Make 4 Side Units.
   - Piece feather rows as shown. Then, stitch feather rows to outside triangles using partial seams (stitch only where indicated by heavy lines).
   - Join #10 shapes to Side Unit as shown.

Side Unit
Make 4

4. Make 4 Corner Units.
   - Stitch single Light triangles to small diamonds as shown to make 8 units. Four of these units will be the reverse of the other 4.

Make 4 each

   - Complete feather rows and join to corner squares.

Corner Unit
Make 4

5. Make one Center Unit.
6. Join sewn units together in rows. Stitch seams in order indicated below by heavy lines to complete partial seams.
7. Cut an 8" circle from freezer paper. Turn the edges of the pieced center circle over the edges of the paper and press. Pin circle in place and appliqué.

Center Unit
Make 1

FEATHERED STAR QUILT BLOCKS I 37

Alternatives
Additional colorations and design ideas.

Cutting Chart
At the top, you'll find the finished size of the block design. Some blocks are given in more than one size. There will be a separate Cutting Chart for each size. Cutting information is in seven main columns:

- **Fabric** - These are the light, medium and dark values used in the block.
- **Shape** - Drawings of the different shapes to be cut.
  NT means NO TEMPLATE is given because the shapes are too large for the page format in the book.
- **Template #** - The template designations refer to the actual templates that begin on page 48. Half-square triangle labels start with T. Quarter-square triangles start with TT. Squares start with S; kites, with K; octagons, with O; diamonds, with a D and special templates have numbers.
- **Number Needed** - Tells how many of this shape and value are needed for the block as shown on the upper left of the page.
- **Squares to Cut** - If cutting the shape begins with a square, this tells how many squares to cut.
- **Cut Size** - Gives square dimensions. See page 9 for an explanation of the little "+" sign after some dimensions.
- **Additional Cuts** - Shows how to cut the square. Page numbers refer to further special cutting instructions.

FEATHERED LE MOYNE STAR

This old-fashioned Feathered Star is offered in both 12" and 15" sizes. The piecing involves partial and set-in seams, so be sure to read about these techniques in the General Piecing on page 16 before you begin. Also refer to How to Piece the Le Moyne Star on page 17.

If you make the 12" version, watch for the little "+" signs that tell you to cut the dimension given plus 1/16"!

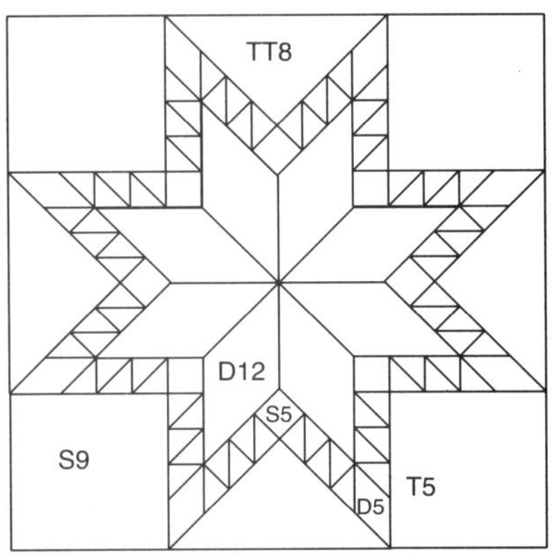

Bias-Strip Piecing (See p. 12)

- Cut 2"-wide bias strips from Light and Medium 12" squares.
- Cut 32 Feather Squares, 1-1/2" x 1-1/2" (S5).

Cutting Chart: 15" finished block

Fabric	Shape	Temp.#	Number Needed	Squares to Cut	Cut Size	Add'l Cut
Light		T5	16	8	1-7/8" x 1-7/8"	
	NT	TT8	4	1	7-1/2" x 7-1/2"	
		S9	4	4	4-7/8" x 4-7/8"	
		D12	4	Cut a strip 2-5/8" wide Make 45° cuts 2-5/8" apart		See p. 11
		Cut one 12" square for bias-strip piecing Feather Triangles				
Medium		S5	8	8	1-1/2" x 1-1/2"	
		D5	8	Cut a strip 1-1/2" wide Make 45° cuts 1-1/2" apart		See p. 11
		Cut one 12" square for bias-strip piecing Feather Triangles				
Dark		D12	4	Cut a strip 2-5/8" wide Make 45° cuts 2-5/8" apart		See p. 11

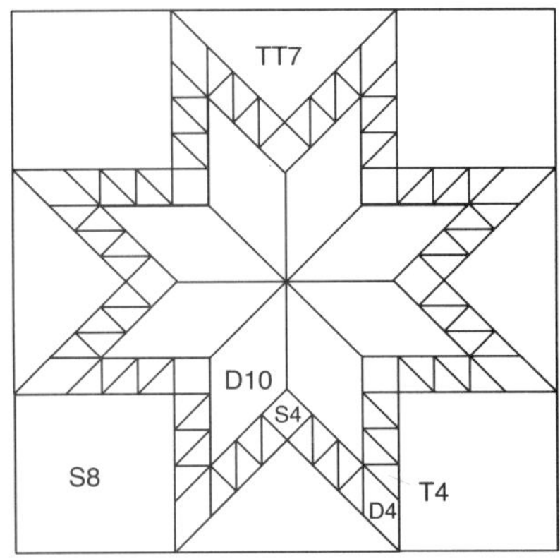

Bias-Strip Piecing (See p. 12)

- Cut 2"-wide bias strips from Light and Medium 10" squares.
- Cut 32 Feather Squares, 1-1/4+" x 1-1/4+" (S4).

Cutting Chart: 12" finished block

Fabric	Shape	Temp.#	Number Needed	Squares to Cut	Cut Size	Add'l Cut
Light		T4	16	8	1-5/8+" x 1-5/8+"	
		TT7	4	1	6-1/4" x 6-1/4"	
		S8	4	4	4" x 4"	
		D10	4	Cut a strip 2-1/8+" wide Make 45° cuts 2-1/8+" apart		See p. 11
		Cut one 10" square for bias-strip piecing Feather Triangles				
Medium		S4	8	8	1-1/4+" x 1-1/4+"	
		D4	8	Cut a strip 1-1/4+" wide Make 45° cuts 1-1/4+" apart		See p. 11
		Cut one 10" square for bias-strip piecing Feather Triangles				
Dark		D10	4	Cut a strip 2-1/8+" wide Make 45° cuts 2-1/8+" apart		See p. 11

Piecing Instructions

1. Cut patches according to Cutting Chart on page 20.

2. Make 32 Feather Squares using bias-strip piecing.

3. Make 4 Side Units.
   - Piece feather rows as shown. Then, stitch feather rows to outside triangles using partial seams (stitch only where indicated by heavy lines).

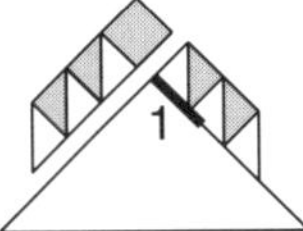

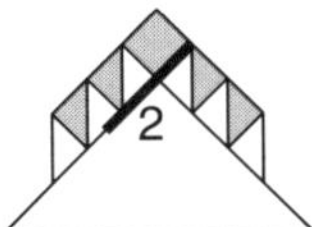

   - Using set-in seam techniques, add large center diamonds to complete units.

Side Unit
Make 4

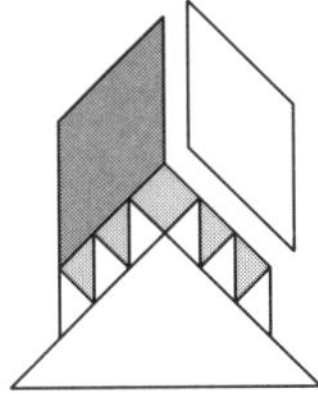

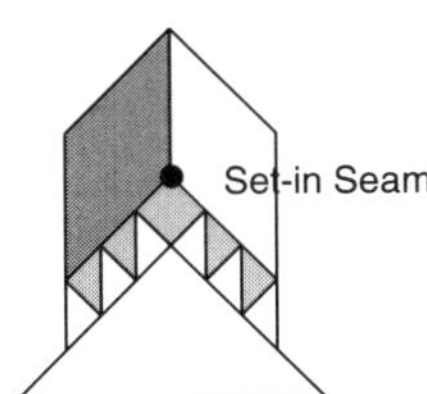

4. Make 4 Corner Units.
   - Stitch single Light triangles to small diamonds as shown to make 8 units. Four of these units will be the reverse of the other 4.

   - Complete feather rows and join to corner squares.

Corner Unit
Make 4

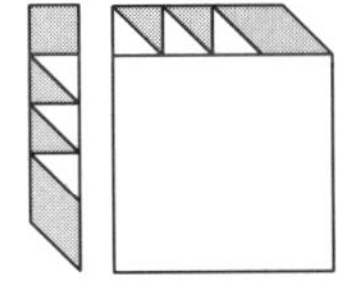

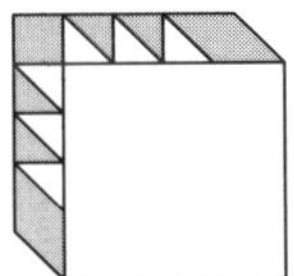

5. Join a Corner Unit to each Side Unit. Starting at the 1/4" seam allowance (dot), stitch seam indicated by #1 first, then complete the partial seam, #2.

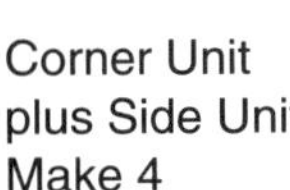

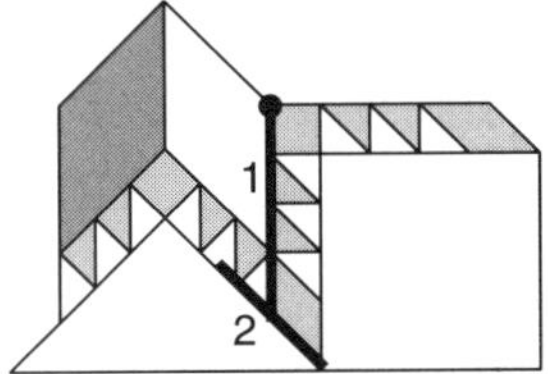

6. Continue joining units together as in Step 5. Make Block "halves" first and then join all together using set-in and partial seams.

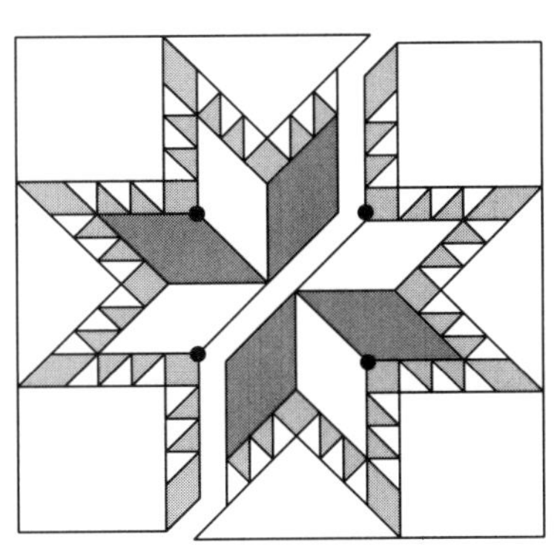

Alternate Shadings

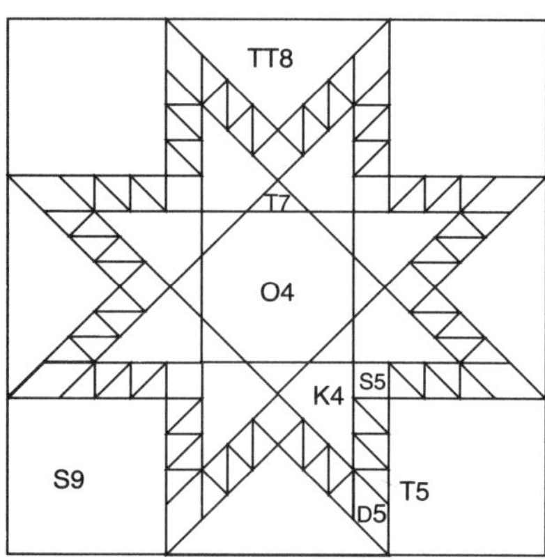

Bias-Strip Piecing (See p. 12)
- Cut 2"-wide bias strips from Light and Medium 12" squares.
- Cut 32 Feather Squares, 1-1/2" x 1-1/2" (S5).

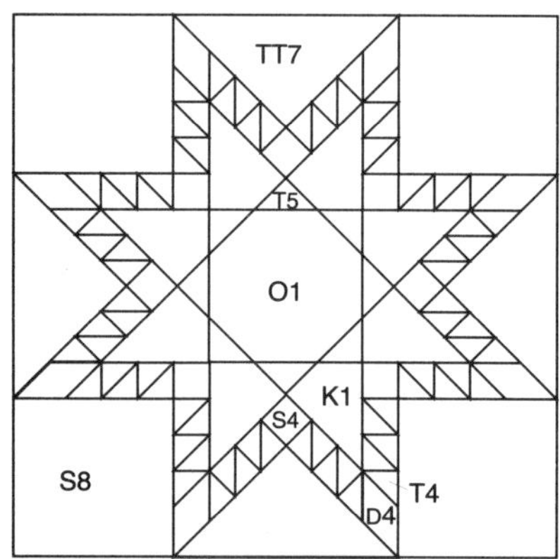

Bias-Strip Piecing (See p. 12)
- Cut 2"-wide bias strips from Light and Medium 10" squares.
- Cut 32 Feather Squares, 1-1/4+" x 1-1/4+" (S4).

RADIANT STAR

Also known as Chestnut Burr, the Radiant Star is offered here in both 12" and 15" sizes. It is one of the easiest Feathered Star blocks to make. The piecing involves partial seams, so be sure to read about this technique in General Piecing on page 16 before you begin. If you make the 12" version, watch for the little "+" signs that tell you to cut the dimension given plus 1/16"!

As a design option, the S5 squares are often replaced with two-triangle Feather Squares.

Cutting Chart: 15" finished block

Fabric	Shape	Temp.#	Number Needed	Squares to Cut	Cut Size	Add'l Cut
Light		T5	16	8	1-7/8" x 1-7/8"	
		T7	8	4	2-1/8" x 2 -1-/8"	
	NT	TT8	4	1	7-1/2" x 7-1/2"	
		S9	4	4	4-7/8" x 4-7/8"	
		Cut one 12" square for bias-strip piecing Feather Triangles				
Medium		K4	8	4	3-7/8" x 3-7/8"	See p.10
		Cut one 12" square for bias-strip piecing Feather Triangles				
Dark		S5	8	8	1-1/2" x 1-1/2"	
		O4	1	1	4-3/4" x 4-3/4"	See p.11
		D5	8		Cut a strip 1-1/2" wide Make 45° cuts 1-1/2" apart	See p. 11

Cutting Chart: 12 " finished block

Fabric	Shape	Temp.#	Number Needed	Squares to Cut	Cut Size	Add'l Cut
Light		T4	16	8	1-5/8+" x 1-5/8+"	
		T5	8	4	1-7/8" x 1-7/8"	
		TT7	4	1	6-1/4" x 6-1/4"	
		S8	4	4	4" x 4"	
		Cut one 10" square for bias-strip piecing Feather Triangles				
Medium		K1	8	4	3-1/4" x 3-1/4"	See p.10
		Cut one 10" square for bias-strip piecing Feather Triangles				
Dark		S4	8	8	1-1/4+" x 1-1/4+"	
		O1	1	1	3-7/8" x 3-7/8"	See p.11
		D4	8		Cut a strip 1-1/4+" wide Make 45° cuts 1-1/4+" apart	See p. 11

Piecing Instructions

1. Cut patches according to Cutting Chart on page 22.

2. Make 32 Feather Squares using bias-strip piecing.

3. Make 4 Side Units.
   - Piece feather rows as shown. Then, stitch feather rows to outside triangles using partial seams (stitch only where indicated by heavy lines).

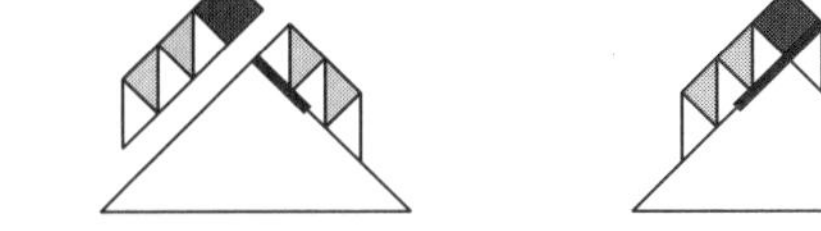

   - Join kite shapes and triangles as shown.

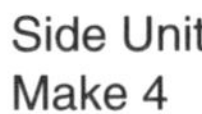

Side Unit
Make 4

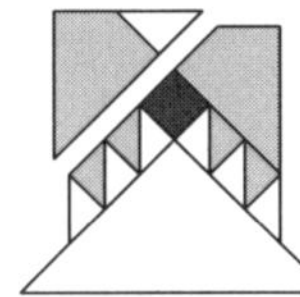

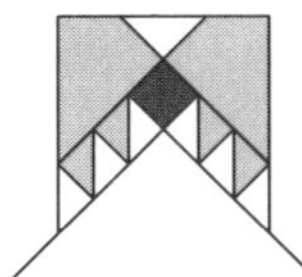

4. Make 4 Corner Units.
   - Stitch single Light triangles to small diamonds as shown to make 8 units. Four of these units will be the reverse of the other 4.

Make 4 each

   - Complete feather rows and join to corner squares.

Corner Unit
Make 4

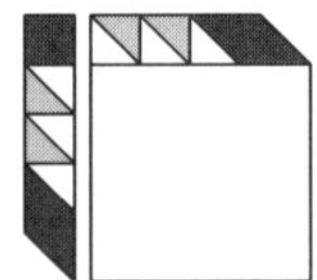

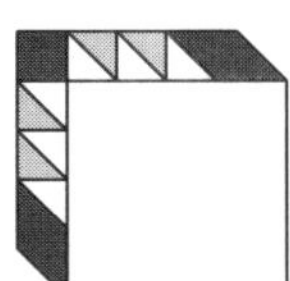

5. Make one Center Unit by stitching a triangle to each bias edge of the octagon.

Center Unit
Make 1

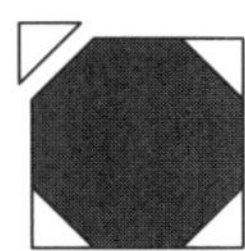

6. Join sewn units together in rows. Stitch seams in order indicated by heavy lines to complete partial seams. Join rows together in same manner to complete the block

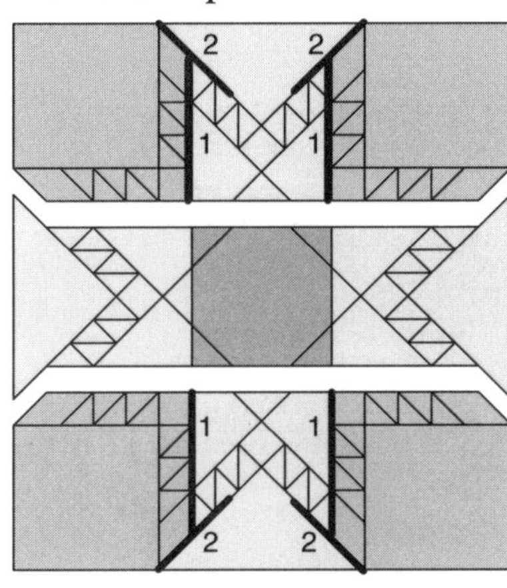

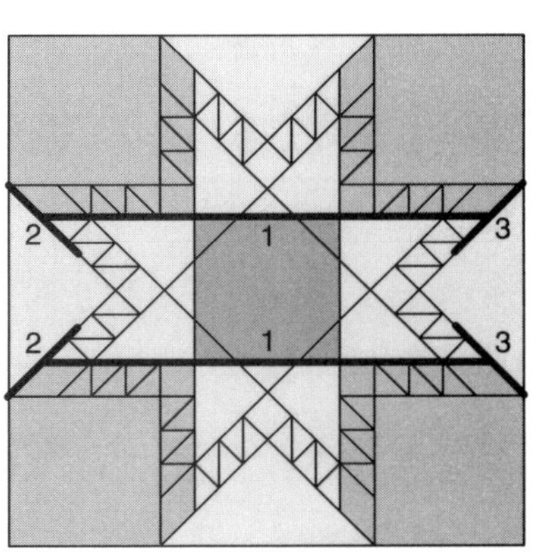

Alternate Shadings

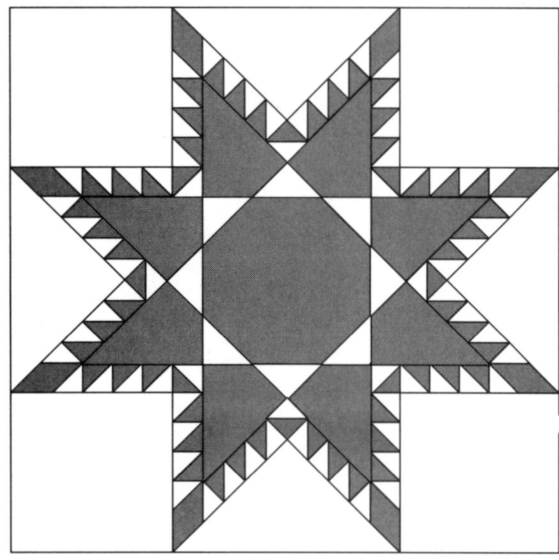

FEATHERED STAR I

This block is similar to the Radiant Star on page 22, only it has more feathers. The piecing involves partial seams, so be sure to read about this technique in General Piecing on page 16 before you begin. Watch for the little "+" sign that tells you to cut the dimension given plus 1/16"!

If you want to replace the center octagon in this design with a Le Moyne Star, use the second Cutting Chart on this page is for cutting and follow the piecing directions given here and on page 17.

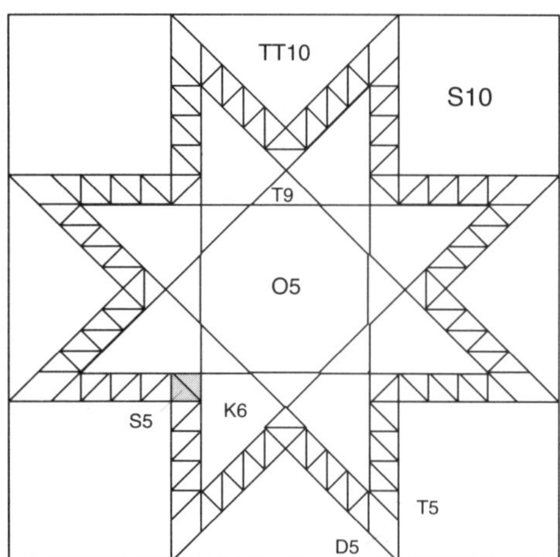

Cutting Chart: 18-1/2" finished block

Fabric	Shape	Temp.#	Number Needed	Squares to Cut	Cut Size	Add'l Cut
Light		T5	16	8	1-7/8" x 1-7/8"	
		T9	8	4	2-1/2" x 2-1/2"	
	NT	TT10	4	1	8-7/8" x 8-7/8"	
	NT	S10	4	4	5-7/8" x 5-7/8"	
		Cut one 13-1/2" square for bias-strip piecing Feather Triangles				
Dark		K6	8	4	4-7/8" x 4-7/8"	See p.10
		Cut one 13-1/2" square for bias-strip piecing Feather Triangles				
		O5	1	1	6-1/8" x 6-1/8"	See p.11
		D5	8	Cut a strip 1-1/2" wide Make 45° cuts 1-1/2" apart		See p. 11

Bias-Strip Piecing (See p. 12)
- Cut 2"-wide bias strips from Light and Dark 13-1/2" squares.
- Cut 56 Feather Squares, 1-1/2" x 1-1/2" (S5).

Cutting Chart: Le Moyne Star Center Variation

Fabric	Shape	Temp.#	Number Needed	Squares to Cut	Cut Size	Add'l Cut
Light		T9	4	2	2-1/2" x 2-1/2"	
		TT2	4	1	3-1/2+" x 3-1/2+"	
Medium		T9	4	2	2-1/2" x 2-1/2"	
		D6	4	Cut a strip 1-5/8+" wide Make 45° cuts 1-5/8+" apart		See p. 11
Dark		D6	4	Cut a strip 1-5/8+" wide Make 45° cuts 1-5/8+" apart		See p. 11

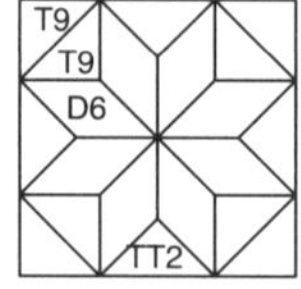

Piecing a Le Moyne Star Center Variation

1. Cut patches according to Cutting Chart above.
2. Refer to Piecing the Le Moyne star on page 17.

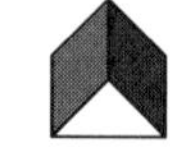

Make 4

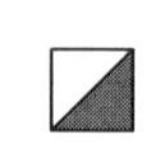

Make 4

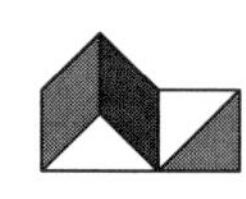

Make 4

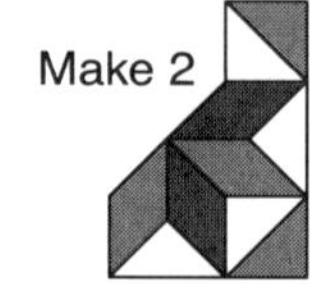

Make 2

Join

Piecing Instructions

1. Cut patches according to Cutting Chart on page 24.

2. Make 56 Feather Squares using bias-strip piecing.

3. Make 4 Side Units.
   - Piece feather rows as shown. Then, stitch feather rows to outside triangles using partial seams (stitch only where indicated by heavy lines).

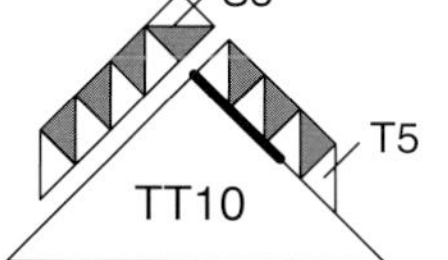

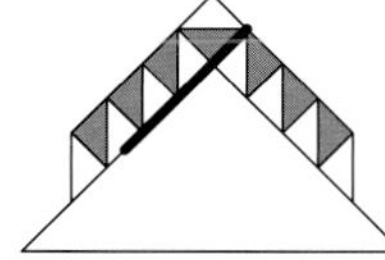

   - Join kite shapes and triangles as shown.

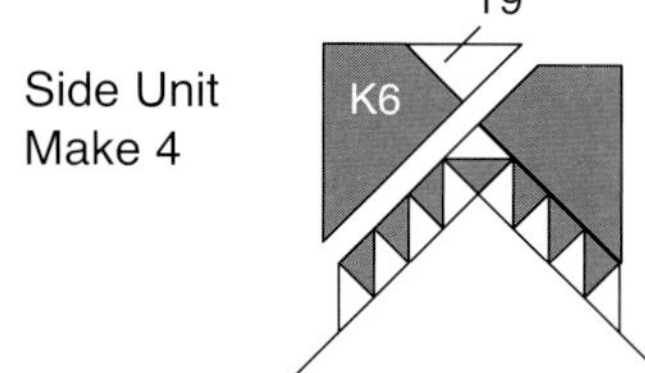

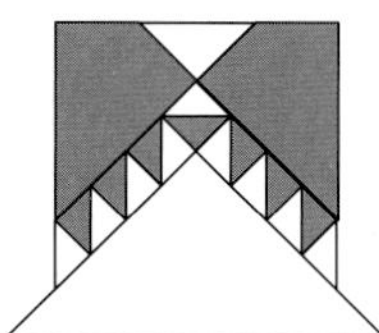

4. Make 4 Corner Units.
   - Stitch single Light triangles to small diamonds as shown to make 8 units. Four of these units will be the reverse of the other 4.

Make 4 each

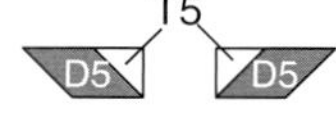

   - Complete feather rows and join to corner squares.

Corner Unit
Make 4

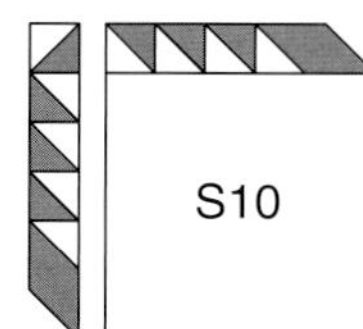

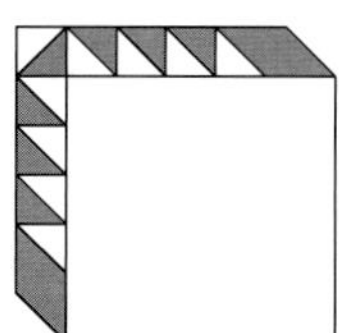

5. Make one Center Unit by stitching a triangle to each bias edge of the octagon.

Center Unit
Make 1

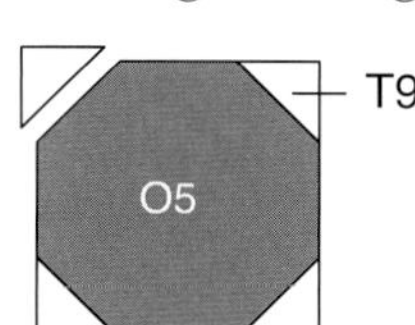

6. Join sewn units together in rows. Stitch seams in order indicated by heavy lines to complete partial seams. Join rows together in same manner to complete the block

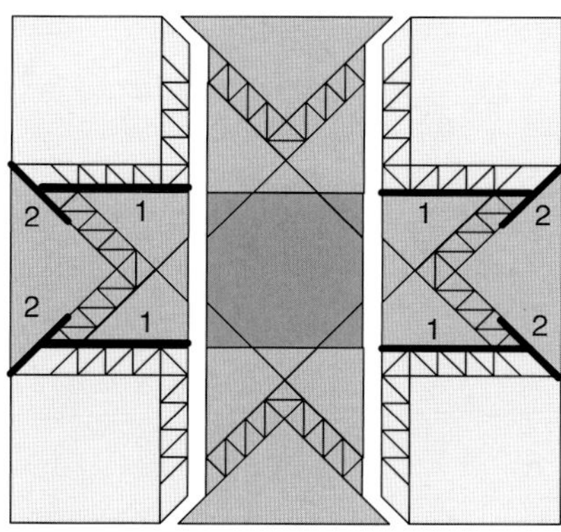

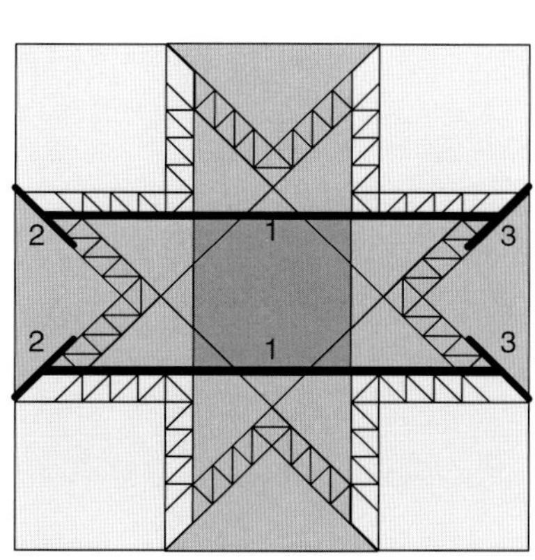

Alternate Shadings

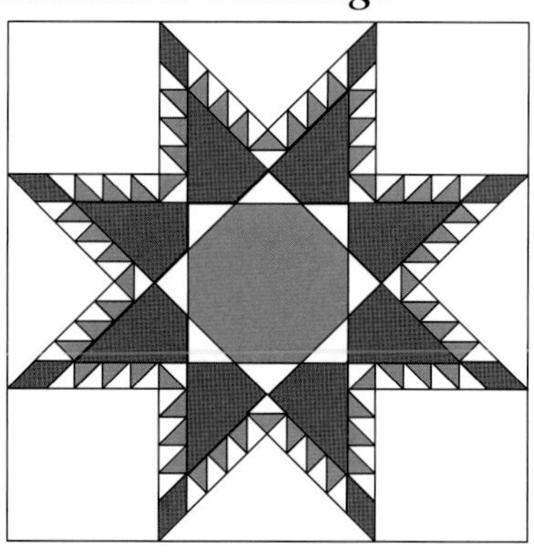
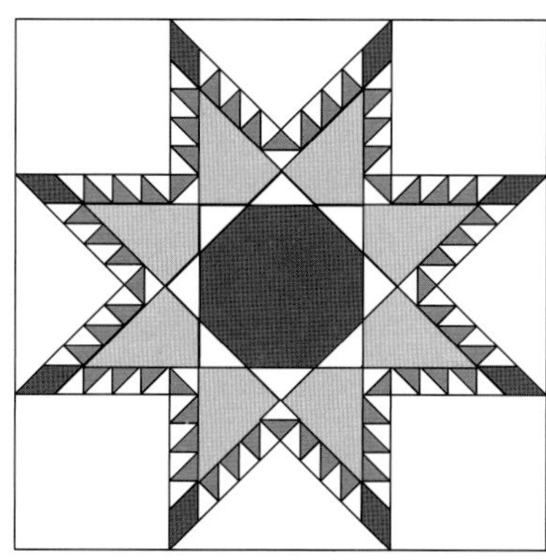

FEATHERED STAR GALLERY

12" and 15" Feathered Le Moyne Star, page 20

12" and 15" Radiant Star, page 22

Radiant Star
by Marsha McCloskey, 1993
Seattle, Washington
72½" x 72½"
Quilted by Freda Smith

Golden Splendor by Marsha McCloskey, 1996 Seattle, Washington 50" x 50". Quilted by Gem Taylor.

18½" Feathered Star I, page 24

21¼" Feathered Star with Mariner's Compass Center (Variation, no pattern given)

Feathered Star with Le Moyne Star Center by Marsha McCloskey, 1998, Seattle, Washington, 40" x 40"

Center Block: 23⅛" and 27½" Feathered Star with Le Moyne Star Center, page 32

Lady of the Lake Feathered Star by Marsha McCloskey, 1996, Seattle, Washington, 40" x 40" Quilted by Gem Taylor

Lady of the Lake Feathered Star Variation made by Joan Hansen

18½" Feathered Star with Reel Center, page 36

18½" Feathered Star with Sunflower Center, page 36

27½" Mexican Pinwheel, page 38

23" Kay's Star, page 40

21¾″ Double Feathered Star, page 42

38″ Triple Feathered Star, page 44

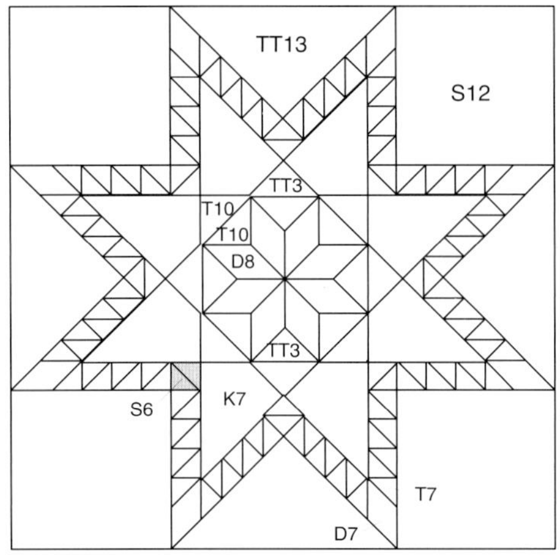

FEATHERED STAR WITH LE MOYNE STAR CENTER

On these two pages are cutting charts for two larger sizes of the same block design given as a center variation on the Feathered Star I on page 24. Often quilters like to use the Feathered Star as a center block for a medallion and a larger block is needed. Follow the Piecing Instructions for the Feathered Star I on page 25 substituting a Le Moyne Star center for the octagon center. The piecing involves partial seams, so be sure to read about this technique in General Piecing on page 16 before you begin. Watch for the little "+" sign that tells you to cut the dimension given plus 1/16"!

Cutting Chart: 23-1/8" finished block

Fabric	Shape	Temp.#	Number Needed	Squares to Cut	Cut Size	Add'l Cut
Light		T7	16	8	2-1/8" x 2-1/8"	
	NT	TT13	4	1	10-7/8" x 10-7/8"	
	NT	S12	4	4	7-1/4" x 7-1/4"	
		Cut one 14" square for bias-strip piecing Feather Triangles				
		T10	4	2	3" x 3"	
		TT3	4	1	4-1/8" x 4-1/8"	
Light 2		T10	4	2	3" x 3"	
		TT3	4	1	4-1/8" x 4-1/8"	
Medium		K7	8	4	5-7/8" x 5-7/8"	See p.10
		D7	8	Cut a strip 1-3/4" wide Make 45° cuts 1-3/4" apart		See p. 11
		D8	4	Cut a strip 2" wide Make 45° cuts 2" apart		See p. 11
Dark		D8	4	Cut a strip 2" wide Make 45° cuts 2" apart		See p. 11
		Cut one 14" square for bias-strip piecing Feather Triangles				

Bias-Strip Piecing (See p. 12)

- Cut 2"-wide bias strips from Light and Dark 14" squares.
- Cut 56 Feather Squares, 1-3/4" x 1-3/4" (S6).

Alternate Shadings

Cutting Chart: 27-1/2" finished block

Fabric	Shape	Temp.#	Number Needed	Squares to Cut	Cut Size	Add'l Cut
Light		T8	16	8	2-3/8" x 2-3/8"	
	NT	TT14	4	1	12-3/4" x 12-3/4"	
	NT	S13	4	4	8-5/8" x 8-5/8"	
		Cut two 14" squares for bias-strip piecing Feather Triangles				
		T11	4	2	3-1/4+" x 3-1/4+"	
		TT4	4	1	4-3/4" x 4-3/4"	
Light 2		T11	4	2	3-1/4+" x 3-1/4+"	
		TT4	4	1	4-3/4" x 4-3/4"	
Medium		K8	8	4	6-7/8" x 6-7/8"	See p.10
		D8	8		Cut a strip 2" wide Make 45° cuts 2" apart	See p. 11
		D11	4		Cut a strip 2-1/4" wide Make 45° cuts 2-1/4" apart	See p. 11
Dark		D11	4		Cut a strip 2-1/4" wide Make 45° cuts 2-1/4" apart	See p. 11
		Cut two 14" squares for bias-strip piecing Feather Triangles				

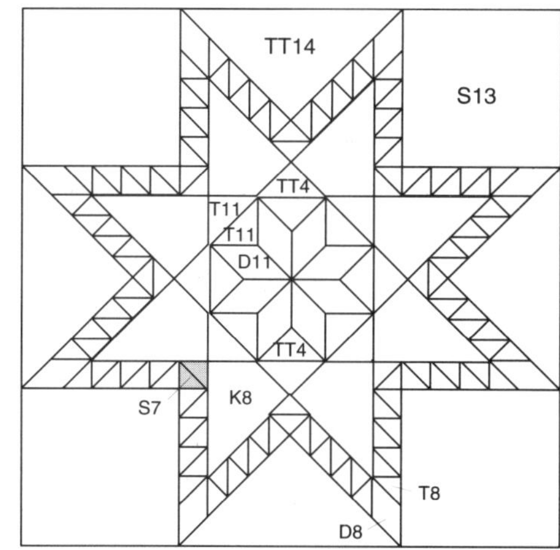

Bias-Strip Piecing (See p. 12)
- Cut 2"-wide bias strips from Light and Dark 14" squares.
- Cut 56 Feather Squares, 2" x 2" (S7).

GRAINLINE TIP

All the triangles in the Le Moyne Star center block are the same size, but are cut differently for grainline placement. The **General Rule** for grainline is that straight grain should fall on the outside edge of the pieced unit or block. Therefore, the triangles cut for the side of the block (A) are cut as quarter-square triangles and have straight grain on the long side. Triangles cut to piece the corner squares (B) are cut as half-square triangles and have straight grain on the short side.

Following the same rule, the same size triangle pieced into the Side Units of these Feathered Star blocks is a quarter-square triangle (A).

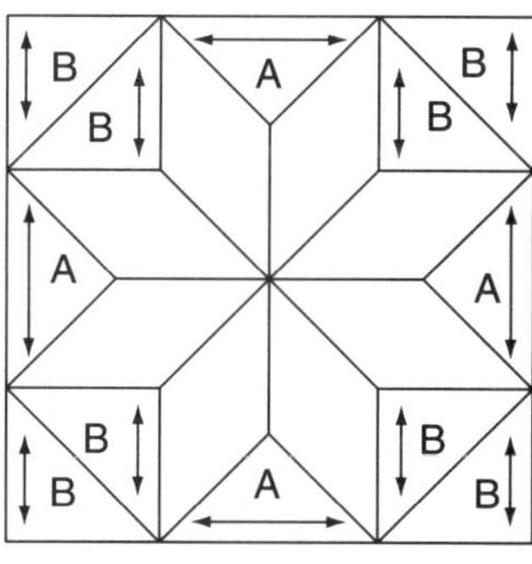

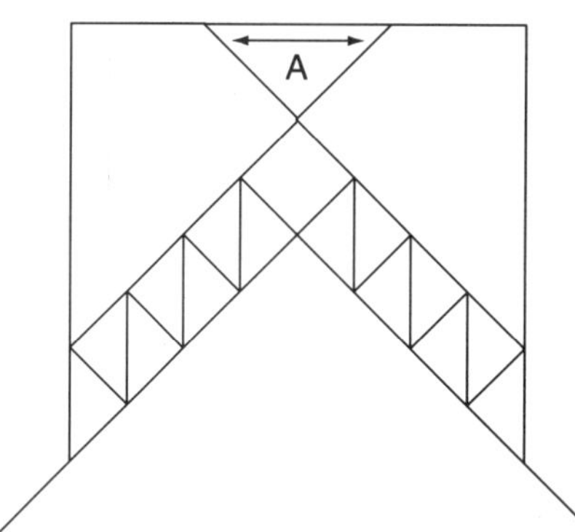

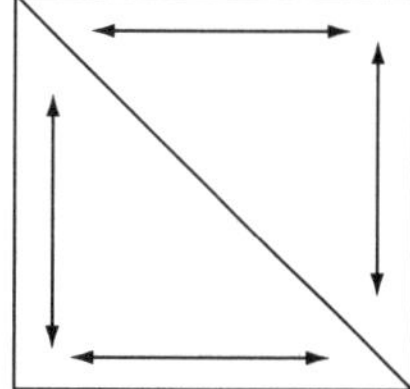

Half-square triangles have straight grain on the short side.

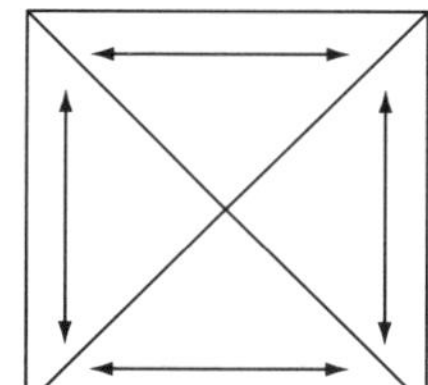

Quarter-square triangles have straight grain on the long side.

LADY OF THE LAKE FEATHERED STAR

This Feathered Star was inspired by an old red, white and blue quilt. Though I didn't copy the original block exactly, I was taken with the fact that the feathers went all the way around the corner square making a Lady of the Lake design. One of the wonderful design advantages of Le Moyne-based stars is that the side triangles are equal to half of the corner square. Therefore, the corner squares also fit on the sides, and the block can be expanded evenly as in the Design Idea given on the next page.

The Cutting Chart below gives instructions for multi-colored Feather Squares.

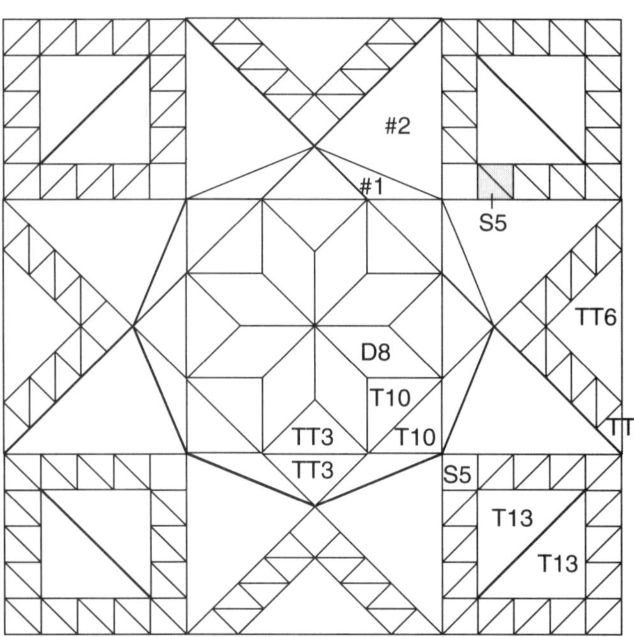

Cutting Chart: 17" finished block

Fabric	Shape	Temp.#	Number Needed	Squares to Cut	Cut Size	Add'l Cut
Light		T10	4	2	3" x 3"	
		TT6	4	1	5-1/2" x 5-1/2"	
		TT1	8	2	2-5/8" x 2-5/8"	
		Cut five 8" squares for bias-strip piecing Feather Triangles				
		T13	4	2	3-7/8" x 3-7/8"	
		TT3	4	1	4-1/8" x 4-1/8"	
Medium 1		T13	4	2	3-7/8" x 3-7/8"	
		D8	4	Cut a strip 2" wide Make 45° cuts 2" apart		See p. 11
		#1	8	Use template on page 57		
Medium 2		TT3	4	1	4-1/8" x 4-1/8"	
		T10	4	2	3" x 3"	
		#2	8	Use template on page 57		
Dark		S5	8	8	1-1/2" x 1-1/2"	
		D8	4	Cut a strip 2" wide Make 45° cuts 2" apart		See p. 11
		Cut five assorted 8" squares for bias-strip piecing Feather Triangles				

Bias-Strip Piecing (See p. 12)
- Cut 2"-wide bias strips from Light and Dark 8" squares.
- Cut 84 Feather Squares, 1-1/2" x 1-1/2" (S5).

Piecing Instructions

1. Cut patches according to Cutting Chart above.

2. Make 84 Feather Squares (S5) using bias-strip piecing.

3. Make one Center Star Unit. Follow the general instructions on page 17 for Piecing the Le Moyne Star. Also see Grainline Tip on page 33.

Center Star Unit
Make 1

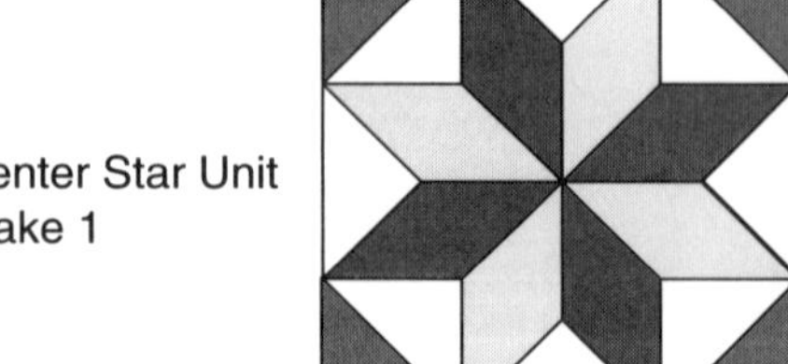

4. Make 4 Side Units.
   - Join #1 and #2 triangles to make 8 kite-shaped units.

   - Piece feather rows as shown. Then, stitch feather rows to TT6 outside triangles .

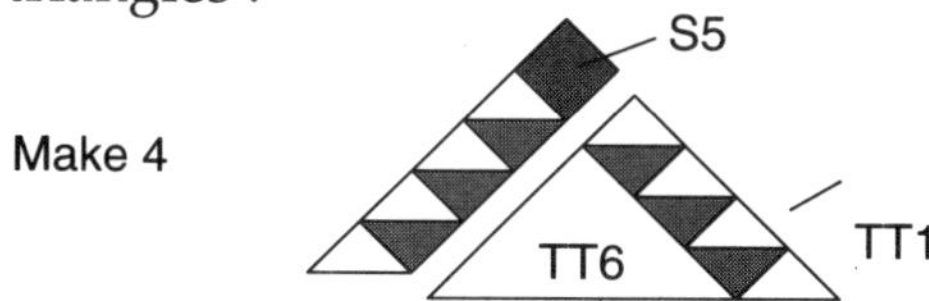

   - Join kite shapes and triangles as shown at right.

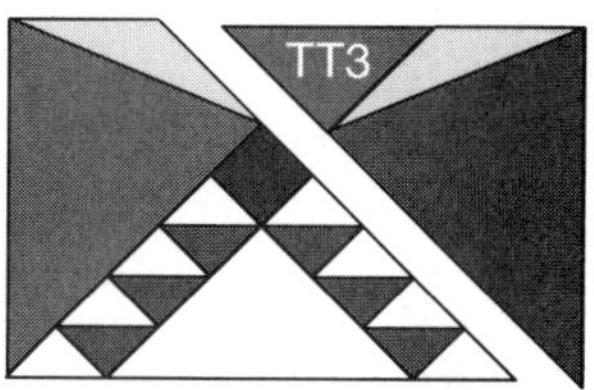

5. Make 4 Corner Units.
   - Stitch T13 triangles together to make 4 squares.

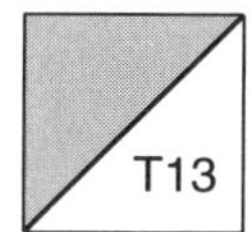

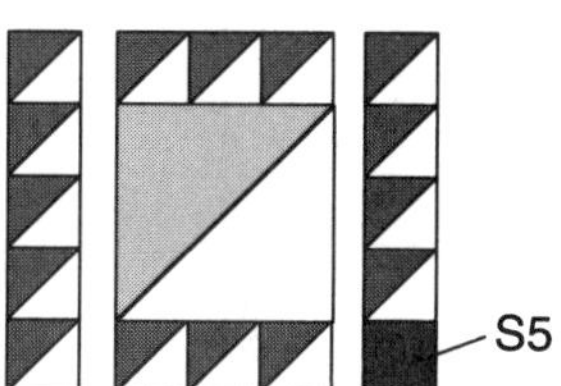

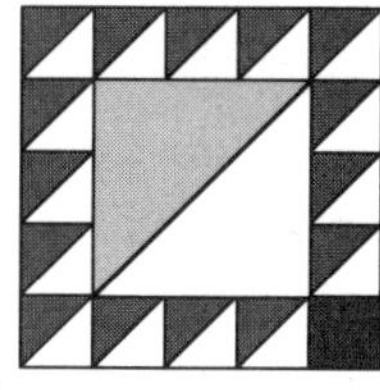

- Complete feather rows and join to T13 unit as shown at right.

6. Join sewn units together in rows. Stitch rows together to complete the block.

Design Idea

FEATHERED STAR WITH REEL CENTER

The design secret of this block is that the center circle has a diameter of 8" finished: large enough for a sunflower or Mariner's Compass. These days such circular designs are easy to make with paper foundation piecing. Space doesn't allow for giving all the possible patterns here, but if you are proficient at drafting, the possibilities are pretty exciting. To draw the Mariner's Compass center pictured below, I referred to Judy Mathieson's book, *Mariner's Compass Quilts: New Directions.*

To make the circular Reel or Sunflower centers, you'll need to make stiffened templates of the curved shapes found on pages 56 and 57. Trace around the templates and cut with scissors in the traditional manner, or carefully cut around each template with a rotary cutter. I pieced the circle then pieced it into the center of the pieced block. I can see appliqué as a good alternative.

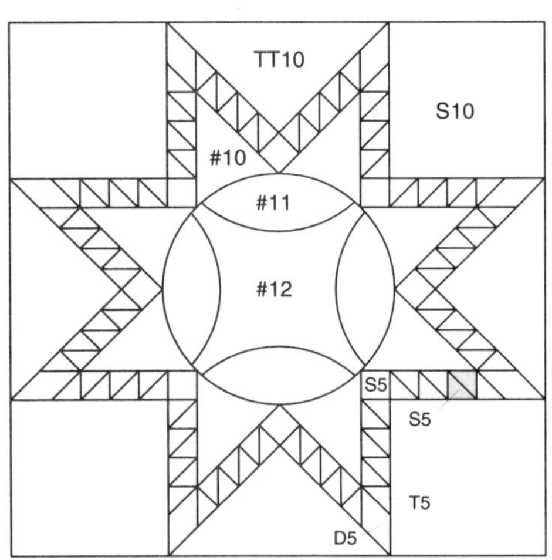

Cutting Chart: 18-1/2" finished block

Fabric	Shape	Temp.#	Number Needed	Squares to Cut	Cut Size	Add'l Cut
Light		#11	4	Make a stiffened template for this curved patch. See above.		
		T5	16	8	1-7/8" x 1-7/8"	
	NT	TT10	4	1	8-7/8" x 8-7/8"	
		S10	4	4	5-7/8" x 5-7/8"	
		Cut one 12" square for bias-strip piecing Feather Triangles				
Medium		S5	8	8	1 1/2" x 1 1/2"	
		Cut one 12" square for bias-strip piecing Feather Triangles				
Dark		D5	8	Cut a strip 1-1/2" wide Make 45° cuts 1-1/2" apart		See p. 11
		#10	8	Make a stiffened template for this curved patch. See above.		
		#12	1	Make a stiffened template for this curved patch. See above.		

Bias-Strip Piecing (See p. 12)
- Cut 2"-wide bias strips from Light and Dark 12" squares.
- Cut 48 Feather Squares, 1-1/2" x 1-1/2" (S5).

Alternatives

Piecing Instructions

1. Cut patches according to Cutting Chart on page 36.

2. Make 48 Feather Squares (S5) using bias-strip piecing.

3. Make 4 Side Units.
   - Piece feather rows as shown. Then, stitch feather rows to outside triangles using partial seams (stitch only where indicated by heavy lines).

   - Join #10 shapes to Side Unit as shown.

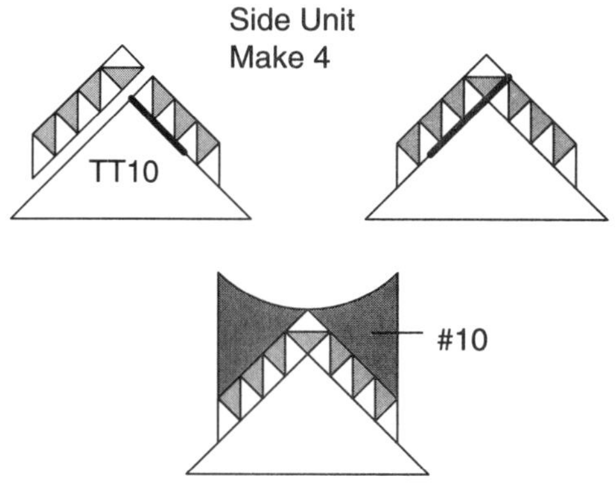

4. Make 4 Corner Units.
   - Stitch single Light triangles to small diamonds as shown to make 8 units. Four of these units will be the reverse of the other 4.

Make 4 each

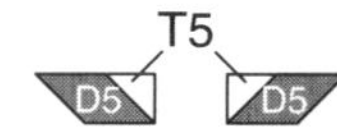

   - Complete feather rows and join to corner squares.

Corner Unit
Make 4

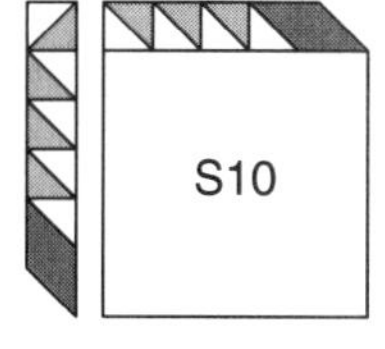

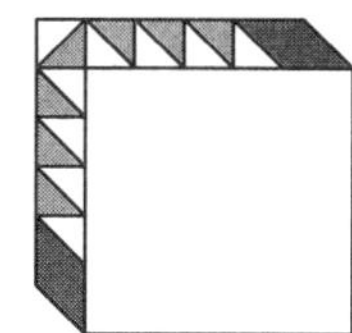

5. Make one Center Unit.

6. Join sewn units together in rows. Stitch seams in order indicated below by heavy lines to complete partial seams.

7. Cut an 8" circle from freezer paper. Turn the edges of the pieced center circle over the edges of the paper and press. Pin circle in place and appliqué.

Center Unit
Make 1

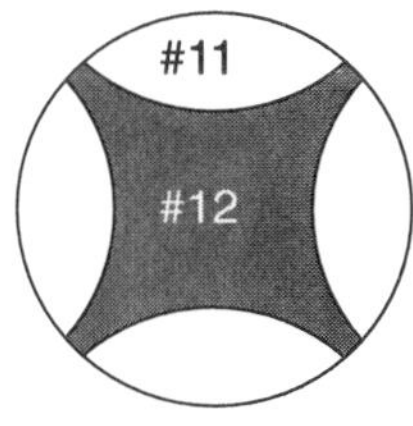

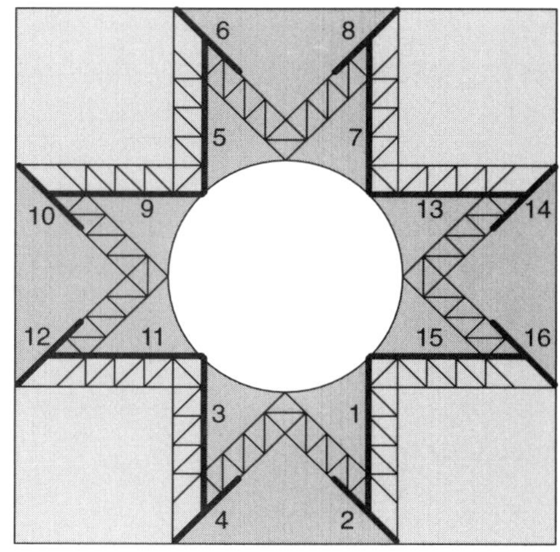

MEXICAN PINWHEEL

This is a large block with plenty of interest and action: a good candidate for the center of a medallion quilt. There are two sets of feathers in this coloring of the Mexican Pinwheel, so a separate set of bias strips is made for each color. The piecing involves lots of partial seams, so be sure to read about this technique in General Piecing on page 16 before you begin.

To help decide on color placement, try photocopying the line drawing on this page. Enlarge the drawing on the copier, and use colored pencils to play with different color combinations.

Cutting Chart: 27-1/2" finished block

Fabric	Shape	Temp.#	Number Needed	Squares to Cut	Cut Size	Add'l Cut
Light		T8	16	8	2-3/8" x 2-3/8"	
		TT4	8	2	4-3/4" x 4-3/4"	
		TT14	4	1	12-3/4" x 12-3/4"	
		S13	4	4	8-5/8" x 8-5/8"	
		Cut **two** 14" squares for bias-strip piecing Feather Triangles				
Med.1		TT9	8	2	7-5/8" x 7-5/8"	
Medium 2		D8	4	Cut a strip 2" wide Make 45° cuts 2" apart		See p. 11
		D11	4	Cut a strip 2-1/4" wide Make 45° cuts 2-1/4" apart		See p. 11
		T8	4	2	2-3/8" x 2-3/8"	
		Cut one 14" square for bias-strip piecing Feather Triangles				
Dark		T8	4	2	2-3/8" x 2-3/8"	
		D8	4	Cut a strip 2" wide Make 45° cuts 2" apart		See p. 11
		D11	4	Cut a strip 2-1/4" wide Make 45° cuts 2-1/4" apart		See p. 11
		Cut one 14" square for bias-strip piecing Feather Triangles				

Bias-Strip Piecing (See p. 12)
- Make 2 sets of 14" squares: Light/Medium 2 and Light/Dark.
- Cut 2"-wide bias strips.
- Cut 40 Feather Squares, 2" x 2" (S7) from each color set (80 total).

Piecing Instructions

1. Cut patches according to Cutting Chart above.

2. Make 40 Feather Squares of the Light/Medium combination and 40 of the Light/Dark using bias-strip piecing.

3. Make 4 Side Units.
  - Stitch single Light triangles (T8) to Medium diamonds (D8) as shown to make 4 units.

Make 4 D8 T8

  - Piece feather rows as shown. The long row includes 7 Light/Medium Feather Squares, one Medium T8 triangle and a diamond/triangle unit. The short row includes 3 Light/Dark Feather Squares and 1 Light T8 triangle. Stitch one TT9 triangle to the short Feather row as shown.

  - Stitch feather rows to the outside triangle (TT14) using one partial seam and one edge-to-edge seam in the order shown.

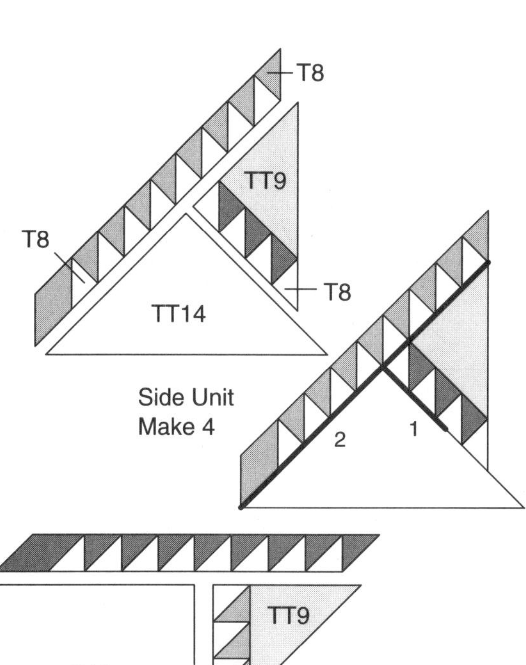

4. Make 4 Corner Units.
  - Stitch single Light triangles (T8) to Dark diamonds (D8) as shown to make 4 units.

Make 4 D8 T8

  - Piece feather rows as shown. The long row includes 7 Light/Dark Feather Squares, one dark T8 triangle and a diamond/triangle unit. The short row includes 3 Light/Medium Feather Squares and 1 Light T8 triangle. Stitch one TT9 triangle to the short Feather row as shown.

  - Stitch feather rows to the Corner square (S13) using one partial seam and one edge-to-edge seam in the order shown.

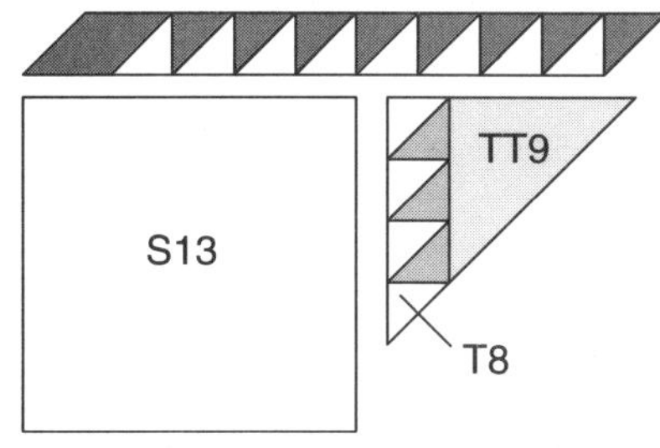

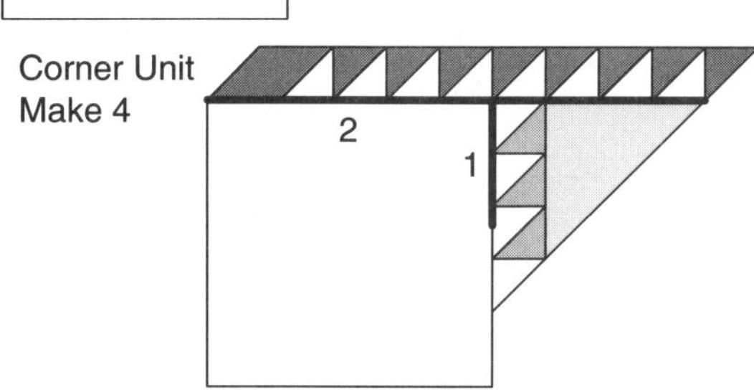

5. Following the general instructions for piecing the Le Moyne Star on page 17, make 1 octagonal star for the Center Unit.

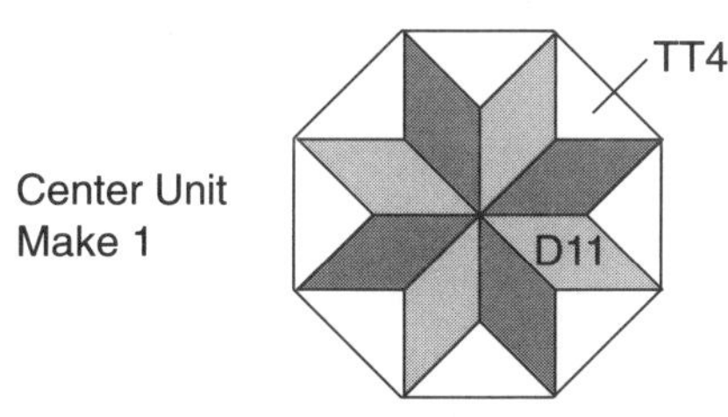

6. Join sewn units together. Stitch seams in order indicated by heavy lines to complete partial seams. Continue until the last partial seams are completed.

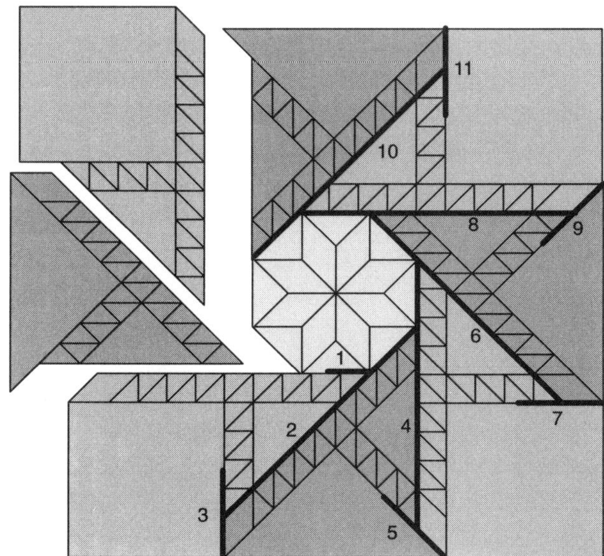

Alternate Shading

KAY'S STAR

This block was designed by Kay Bruce of Kerrville, Texas, after taking taking my Feathered Star drafting class many years ago. It gives the illusion of curved scallops around the center star. It is an easy star to piece. Because there are no partial seams, it is well suited to bar-quilt construction. Watch for the little "+" signs that tell you to cut the dimension given plus 1/16"!

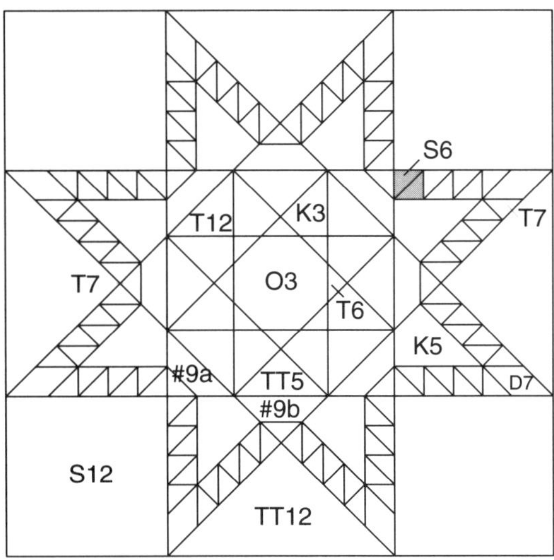

Bias-Strip Piecing (See p. 12)
- Cut 2"-wide bias strips from Light and Dark 14" squares.
- Cut 48 Feather Squares, 1-3/4" x 1-3/4" (S6).

Cutting Chart: 23" finished block

Fabric	Shape	Temp.#	Number Needed	Squares to Cut	Cut Size	Add'l Cut
Light		T7	16	8	2-1/8" x 2-1/8"	
		#9a	4	2	3-5/8" x 3-5/8"	See p.57
		#9b	4	1	5-1/8" x 5-1/8"	See p.57
		T12	4	2	3-5/8" x 3-5/8"	
		TT5	4	1	5-1/8" x 5-1/8"	
		T6	8	4	2" x 2"	
	NT	TT12	4	1	10-3/4" x 10-3/4"	
	NT	S12	4	4	7-1/4" x 7-1/4"	
		Cut one 14" square for bias-strip piecing Feather Triangles				
Dark		T7	8	4	2-1/8" x 2-1/8"	
		K3	8	4	3-5/8" x 3-5/8"	See p.10
		O3	1	1	4-3/8+" x 4-3/8+"	See p.11
		K5	8	4	4-5/8" x 4-5/8"	See p.10
		Cut one 14" square for bias-strip piecing Feather Triangles				
		D7	8		Cut a strip 1-3/4" wide Make 45° cuts 1-3/4" apart	See p. 11

Piecing Instructions

1. Cut patches according to Cutting Chart above.

2. Make 48 Feather Squares (S6) using bias-strip piecing.

3. Make Center Star
   A. Make one Center Unit by stitching a T6 triangle to each bias edge of the O3 Octagon.

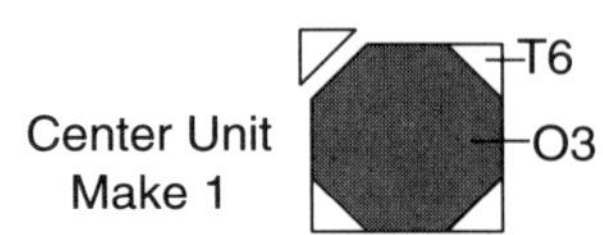

B. Make four Corner Units.

- Make 4 units using Light #9a trapezoids and Dark T7 triangles. (Arrows indicate placement of straight grain.)

- Stitch each unit to T12 Light triangle to make 4 corner squares.

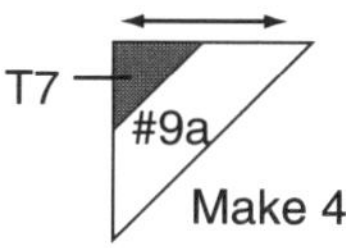

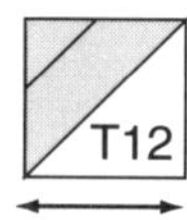

C. Make 4 Star Point Units as shown using TT5 triangles, K3 kites and T6 triangles.

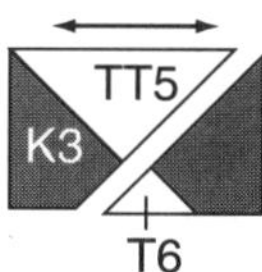

D. To complete the Center Star, stitch the sewn units together in rows as shown, then sew the rows together.

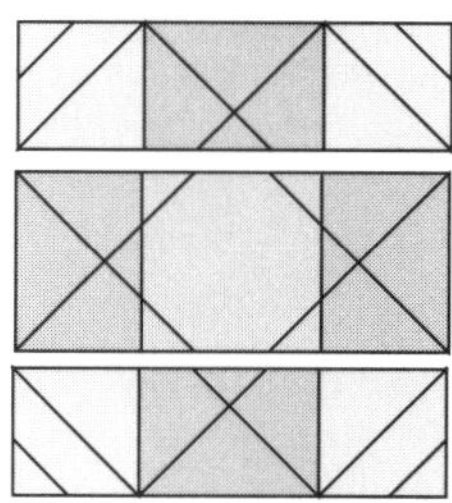

4. Make 4 Side Units

A. Make 4 units using Light #9b trapezoids and Dark T7 triangles. (Arrow indicates placement of straight grain.)

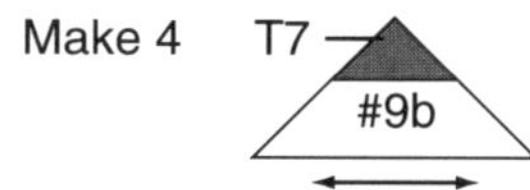

B. Stitch 8 Light T7 triangles to 8 D7 diamonds as shown.

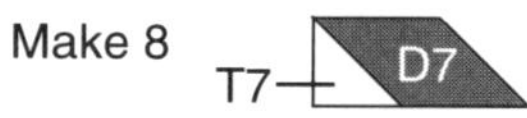

C. Make Feather rows as shown.

D. Join feather rows to K5 Kites as shown to make 8 Feathered Star Point Units.

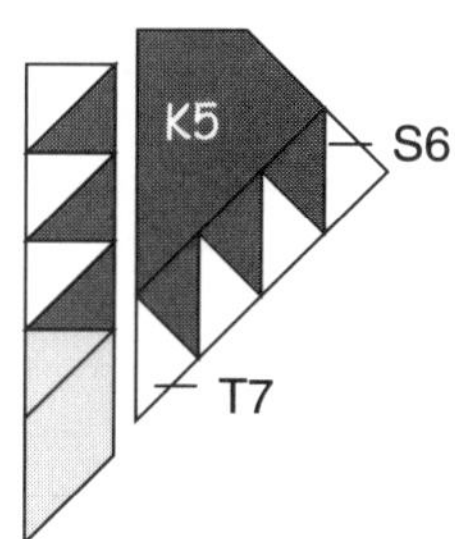

E. Complete 4 Side Units. For each, join 2 Feathered Star Point Units with one unit from step 4 and TT12 triangle.

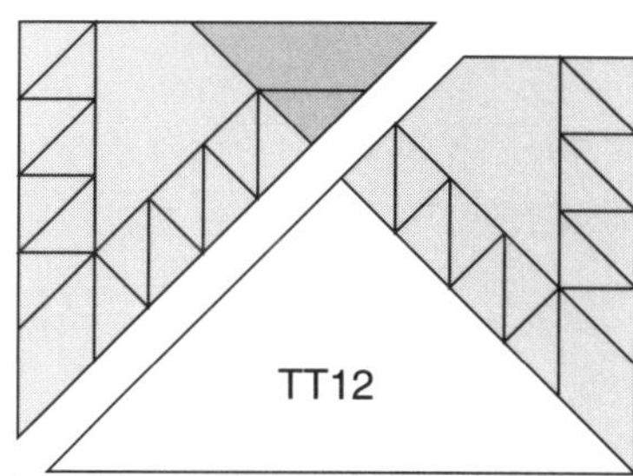

5. To finish the star, join sewn units together with corner S12 squares in rows as shown. Join rows together.

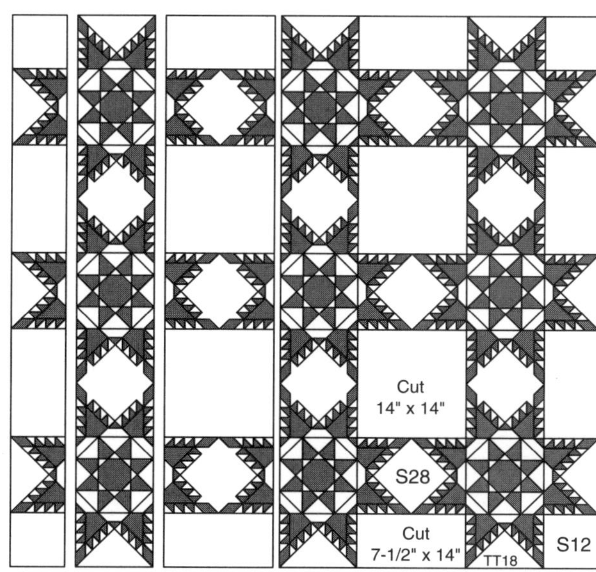

Kay's Stars set together as a Bar Quilt.

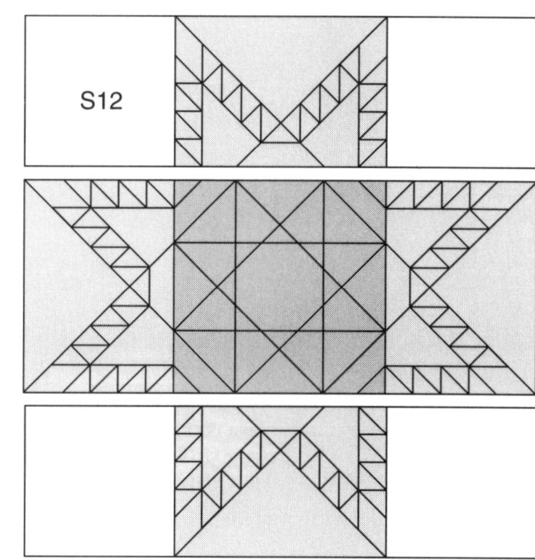

DOUBLE FEATHERED STAR

The delightful version of my Double Feathered Star design shown in the Gallery, was made by Pam Pifer as a test block. My original drawing was a two-color version, but I like her three-fabric rendition better.

This design is pretty demanding because of the tiny Feathers and a multitude of partial seams. Watch for the little "+" signs that tell you to cut the dimension given plus 1/16"! Use your most careful cutting and piecing skills ... and don't hurry!

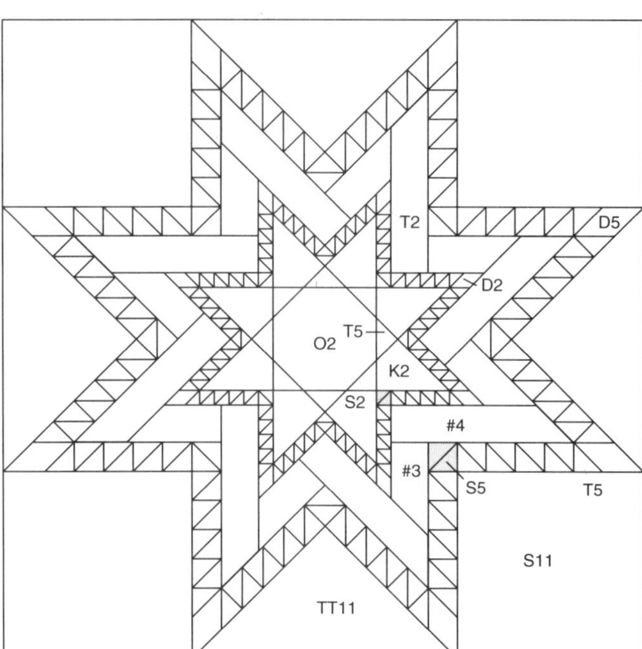

Cutting Chart: 21-3/4" finished block

Fabric	Shape	Temp.#	Number Needed	Squares to Cut	Cut Size	Add'l Cut
Light		T2	16	8	1-3/8" x 1-3/8"	
		T5	8	4	1-7/8" x 1-7/8"	
		D5	8	Cut a strip 1-1/2" wide Make 45° cuts 1-1/2" apart		See p. 11
		#3	8	Cut a rectangle 1-3/4"x 4-1/8" See template, page 55		
		#4	8	Cut a rectangle 1-3/4" x 7-1/8" See template, page 55		
		Cut **two** 14" squares for bias-strip piecing Feather Triangles				
Medium		T5	16	8	1-7/8" x 1-7/8"	
	NT	TT11	4	1	10-1/4" x 10-1/4"	
	NT	S11	4	4	6-7/8" x 6-7/8"	
		Cut one 14" square for bias-strip piecing Feather Triangles				
Dark		D2	8	Cut a strip 1" wide Make 45° cuts 1" apart		See p. 11
		K2	8	4	3-3/8" x 3-3/8"	See p.10
		O2	1	1	4" x 4"	See p.11
		Cut one 14" square for bias-strip piecing Feather Triangles				

Bias-Strip Piecing (See p. 12)
- Cut 2"-wide bias strips from Light and Dark 14" squares.
- Cut 72 Feather Squares, 1" x 1" (S2).
- Cut 2"-wide bias strips from Light and Medium 14" squares.
- Cut 72 Feather Squares, 1-1/2" x 1-1/2" (S5).

Piecing Instructions

1. Cut patches according to Cutting Chart above.

2. Make 72 Feather Squares of each size and color combination using bias-strip piecing.

3. Make Center Star.
   A. Make one Center Unit by stitching a Light T5 triangle to each bias edge of the octagon.

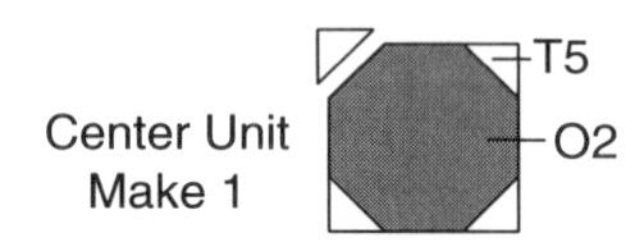

B. Make 8 Unit As. Four of these will become Corner Units and four will have kites and triangles added to make Side Units.

- Stitch single Light T2 triangles to Dark D2 diamonds as shown to make 8. Four of these units will be the reverse of the other 4.

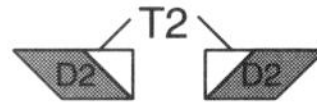

- Piece feather rows as shown.
- Join #3 and #4 patches with a partial seam as shown. Then, stitch feather rows to #3/#4 unit in order with partial seams (stitch only where indicated by heavy lines).

C. Make 4 Side Units

- Join Dark K2s with Light T5 triangles as shown, and join to Feather row units.

D. Join sewn units together to complete the Center Star. Stitch seams in order indicated by heavy lines to complete partial seams.

4. Make 4 Side Units for outside of block.
   - Piece feather rows as shown. Then, stitch feather rows to Medium TT11 triangles using partial seams in the order shown.

5. Make 4 Corner Units for outside of block.
   - Stitch single Medium T5 triangles to Light D5 diamonds to make 8 units. Four of these units will be the reverse of the other 4.

Make 4 each

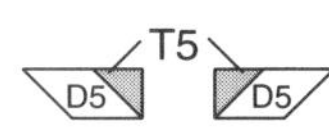

- Complete feather rows and join to corner squares.

6. Join sewn Side Units to Center Star. Stitch seams in order indicated by heavy lines to complete partial seams.

7. Join sewn Corner Units to Center Star. Stitch seams in order indicated by heavy lines to complete partial seams. Join all units together in same manner to complete the block

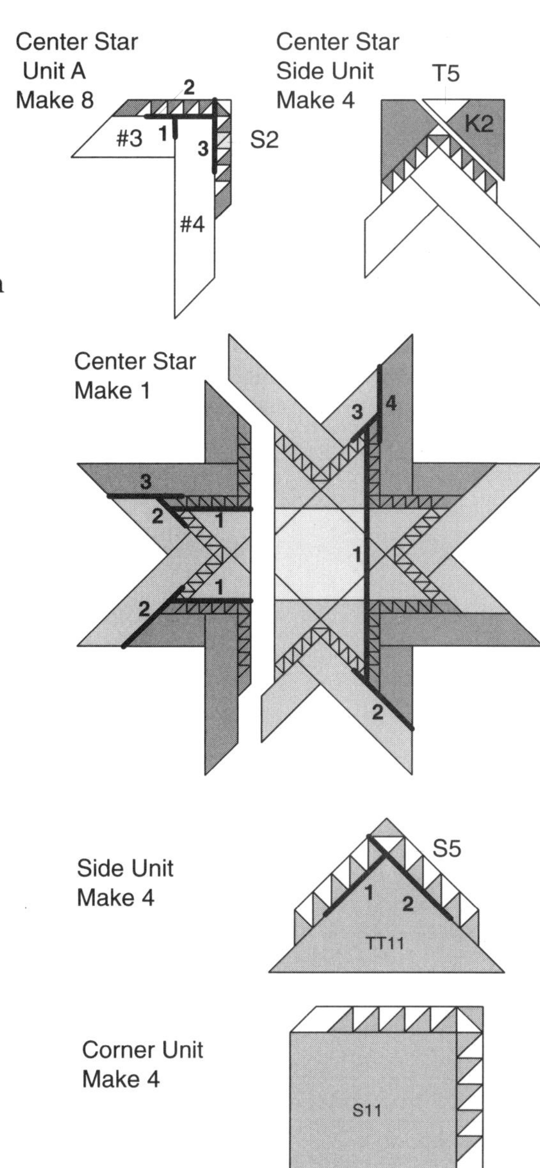

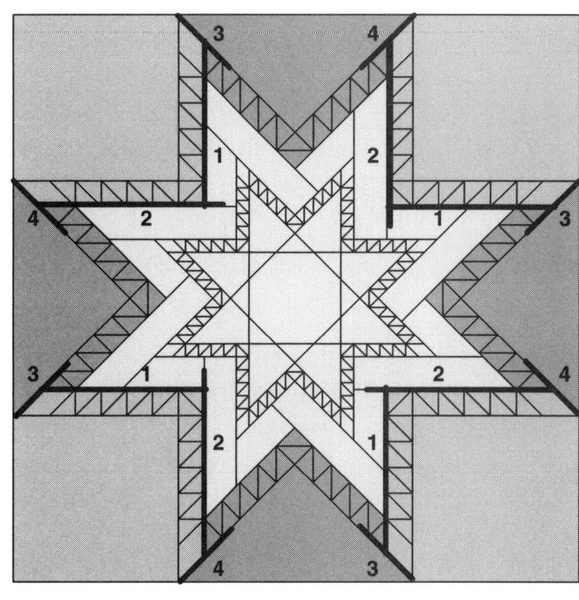

TRIPLE FEATHERED STAR

Hold on to your hats! This block is the hardest one I've ever pieced -- also, the most fun I've had in a long time. It took me 4 days to make the block pictured in the Gallery! To piece this block, you must be comfortable with cutting sixteenths, making miniatures, set-in seams and partial seams. I made it in just two fabrics. If you want to add more color, photocopy the line drawing on this page, enlarge it, and experiment with different colorations.

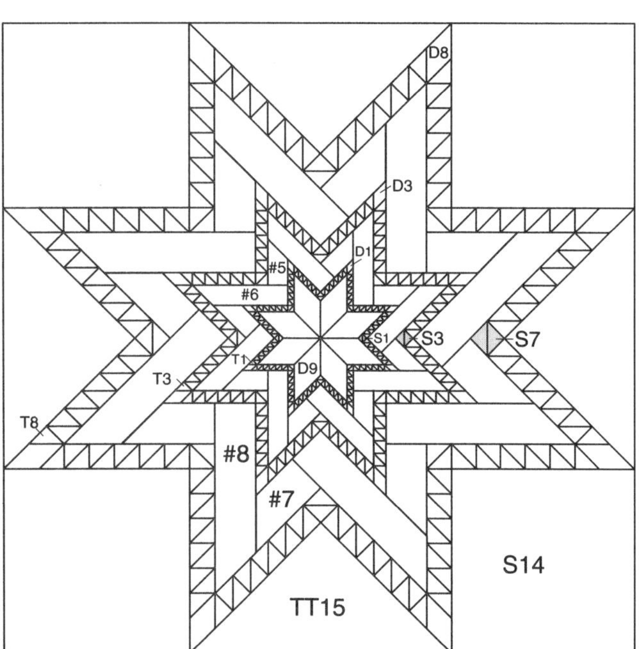

Cutting Chart: 38" finished block

Fabric	Shape	Temp.#	Number Needed	Squares to Cut	Cut Size	Add'l Cut
Light		T1	16	8	1-1/4" x 1-1/4"	
		T3	16	8	1-5/8" x 1-5/8"	
		T8	16	8	2-3/8" x 2-3/8"	
		#5	8	Cut a rectangle 1-5/8+" x 3-5/8" See Template, page 55		
		#6	8	Cut a rectangle 1-5/8+" x 6-1/2+" See Template, page 55		
	NT	TT15	4	1	17" x 17"	
	NT	S14	4	4	11-5/8" x 11-5/8"	
		Cut three 15" squares for bias-strip piecing Feather Triangles				
Dark		D1	8	Cut a strip 7/8" wide Make 45° cuts 7/8" apart		See p. 11
		D3	8	Cut a strip 1-1/4" wide Make 45° cuts 1-1/4" apart		See p. 11
		D8	8	Cut a strip 2" wide Make 45° cuts 2" apart		See p. 11
		D9	8	Cut a strip 2-1/8" wide Make 45° cuts 2-1/8" apart		See p. 11
		#7	8	Cut a rectangle 2-7/8+" x 6-3/8+" See Template, page 55		See p. 10
	NT	#8	8	Cut a rectangle 2-7/8+" x 12-1/4+" See page 55		
		Cut three 15" squares for bias-strip piecing Feather Triangles				

Bias-Strip Piecing (See p. 12)
- Cut 2"-wide bias strips from Light and Dark 15" squares. (This is more than is needed, but allows for extras if you need them.)
- Cut 88 Feather Squares, 7/8" x 7/8" (S1).
- Cut 88 Feather Squares, 1-1/4" x 1-1/4" (S3).
- Cut 88 Feather Squares, 2" x 2" (S7).

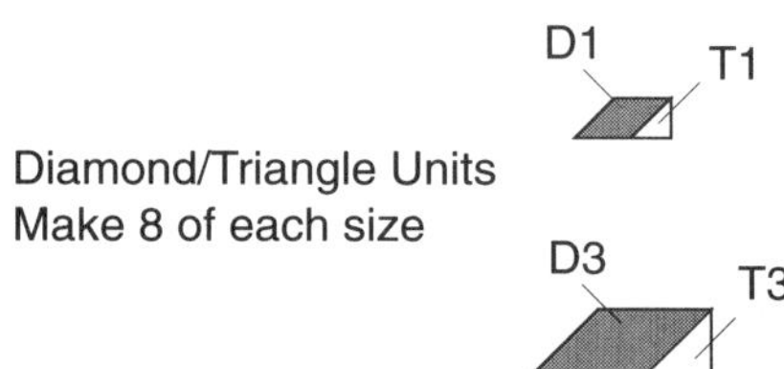

Piecing Instructions

1. Cut patches according to Cutting Chart above.

2. Make 88 Feather Squares of each of 3 sizes using Bias-Strip Piecing. Cut largest units first, then medium, then smallest.

3. Make 8 Diamond/Triangle Units of each size as shown.

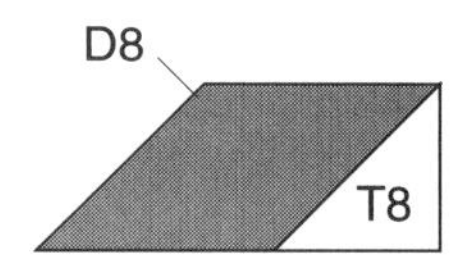

4. Make the Center Star.
   - Join #5 and #6 trapezoids with partial seams as shown to make 8 units. Stitch only where indicated by heavy line.

   - Piece feather rows as shown with S1 Feather Squares, T1 triangles and T1/D1 diamond units. Then, with partial seams, stitch feather rows to previous unit to make 8 Unit 1s.

   - Make 4 Unit 2s. Join 2 D9 diamonds to each of 4 Unit 1s with partial and set-in seams in the order shown. Set-in seams are indicated by a dot: at these points sew only up to the 1/4" seam allowance and backtack.

   - Join Unit 1s and Unit 2s to make 4 Unit 3s with partial and set-in seams in the order shown.

   - Join Unit 3s to make 2 Unit 4s.

   - Join Unit 4s to complete Center Star. Dotted lines indicate remaining partial seams. These are needed in order to add the next round of pieced units.

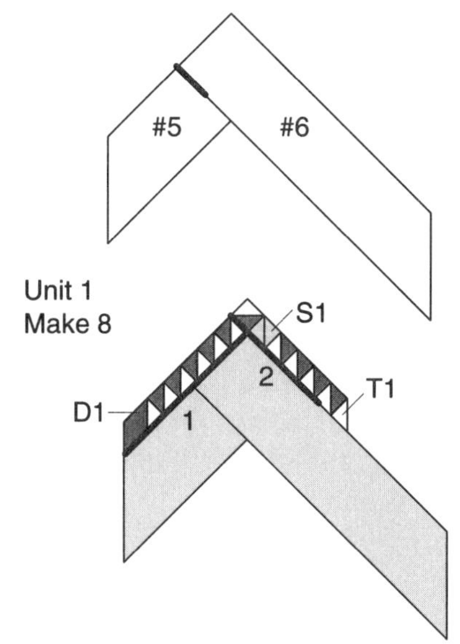

Unit 2
Make 4

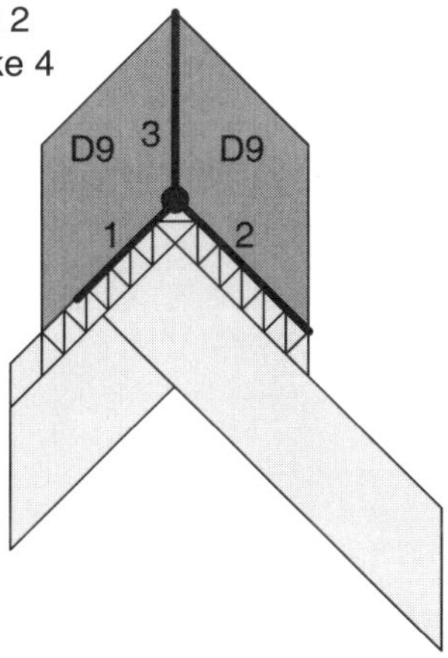

Unit 3
Make 4

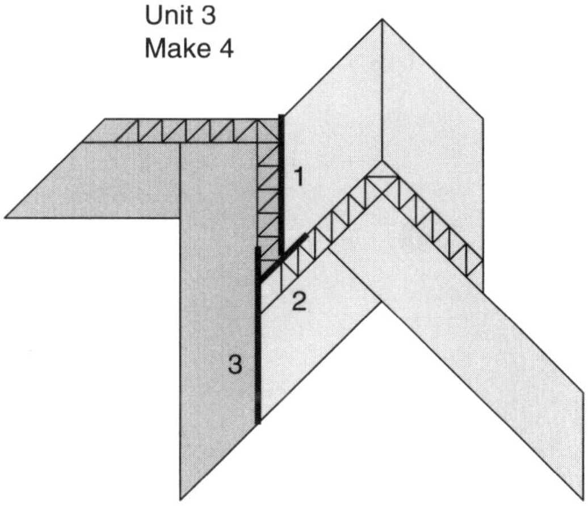

Unit 4
Make 2

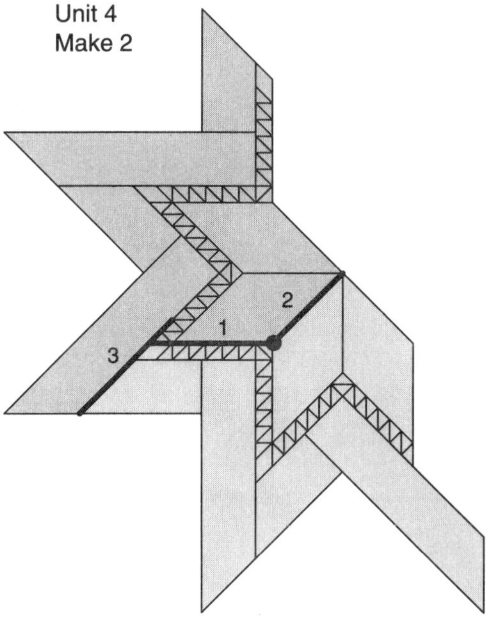

Center Star
Make 1

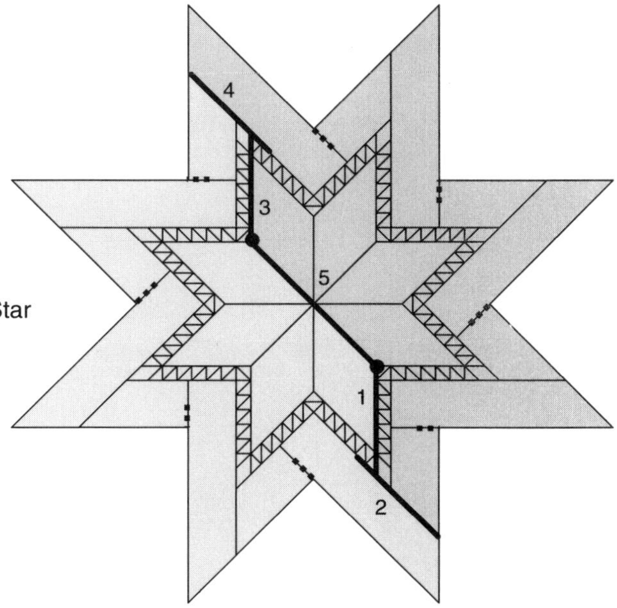

4. Make the Middle Star.
   - Join #7 and #8 trapezoids with partial seams as shown to make 8 units. Stitch only where indicated by heavy line. 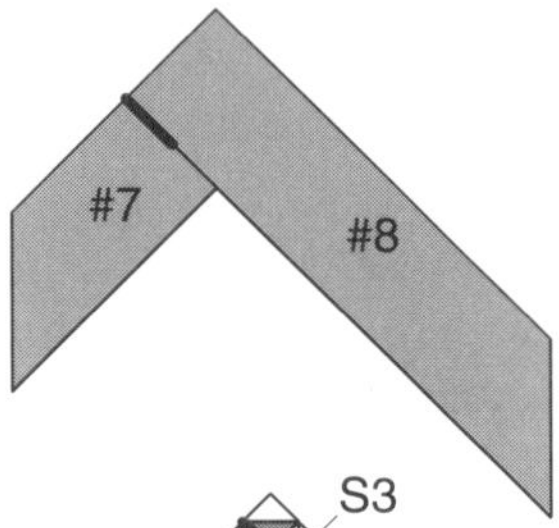
   - Piece feather rows as shown with S3 Feather Squares, T3 triangles and T3/D3 diamond units. Then, with partial seams, stitch feather rows to previous unit to make 8 Unit 5s.
   - Join Unit 5s to Center Star with partial seams in the order shown. Work around the star until all 8 Unit 5s are attached. Dotted lines indicate remaining partial seams. These are needed in order to add the next round of pieced units.

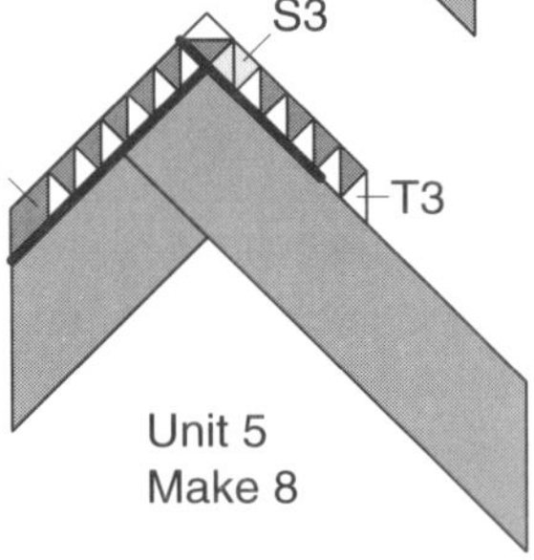

#7
#8

S3
D3
T3

Unit 5
Make 8

1
2

3
1
2

Middle Star
Make 1

6. Make the Outer Star.

• Make 4 of Unit 6. Piece feather rows as shown with S7 Feather Squares, T8 triangles and T8/D8 diamond units. Then, with partial seams in the order shown, stitch feather rows to TT15 triangle.

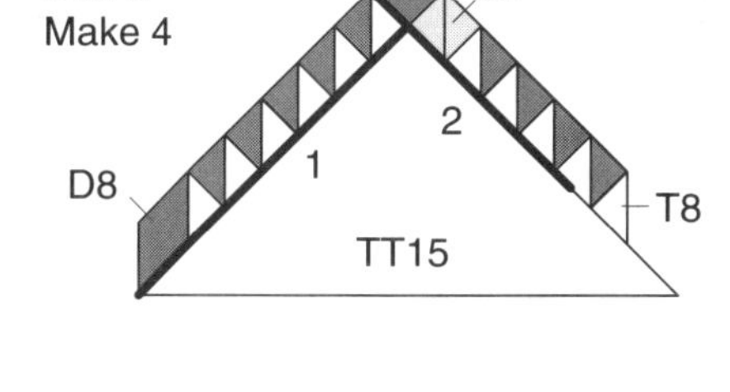

• Make 4 of Unit 7. Piece feather rows as shown with S7 Feather Squares, T8 triangles and T8/D8 diamond units. Then, with partial seams in the order shown, stitch feather rows to S14 square.

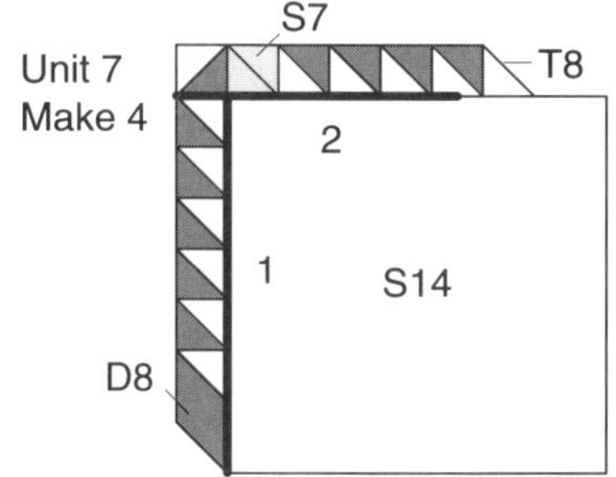

• Join Unit 6s to pieced center with partial seams in the order shown.

• Join Unit 7s to pieced center with partial seams in the order shown. Finish all partial seams and go out on the street and show everyone what you have done!

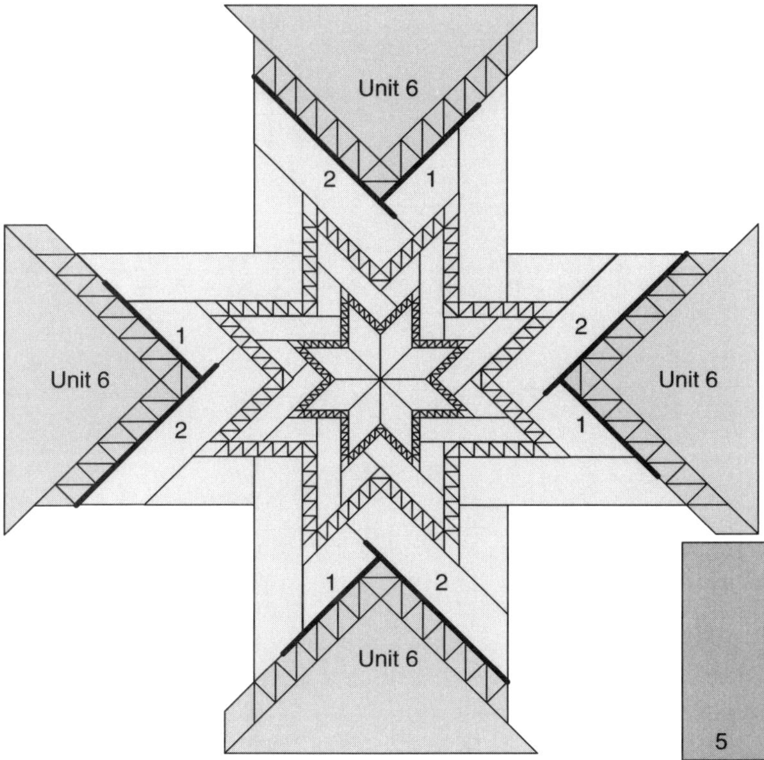

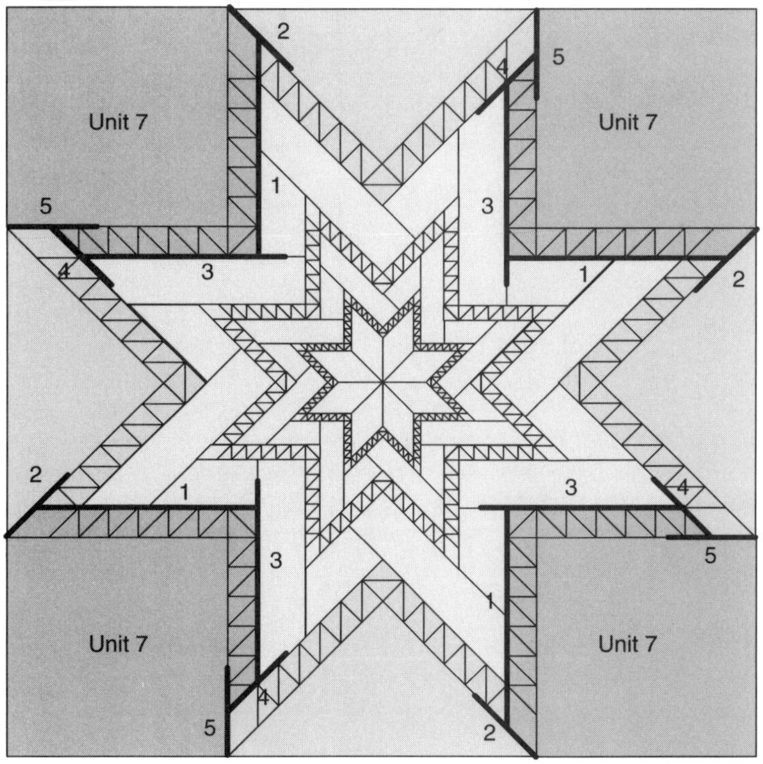

Templates: Diamonds and Kites

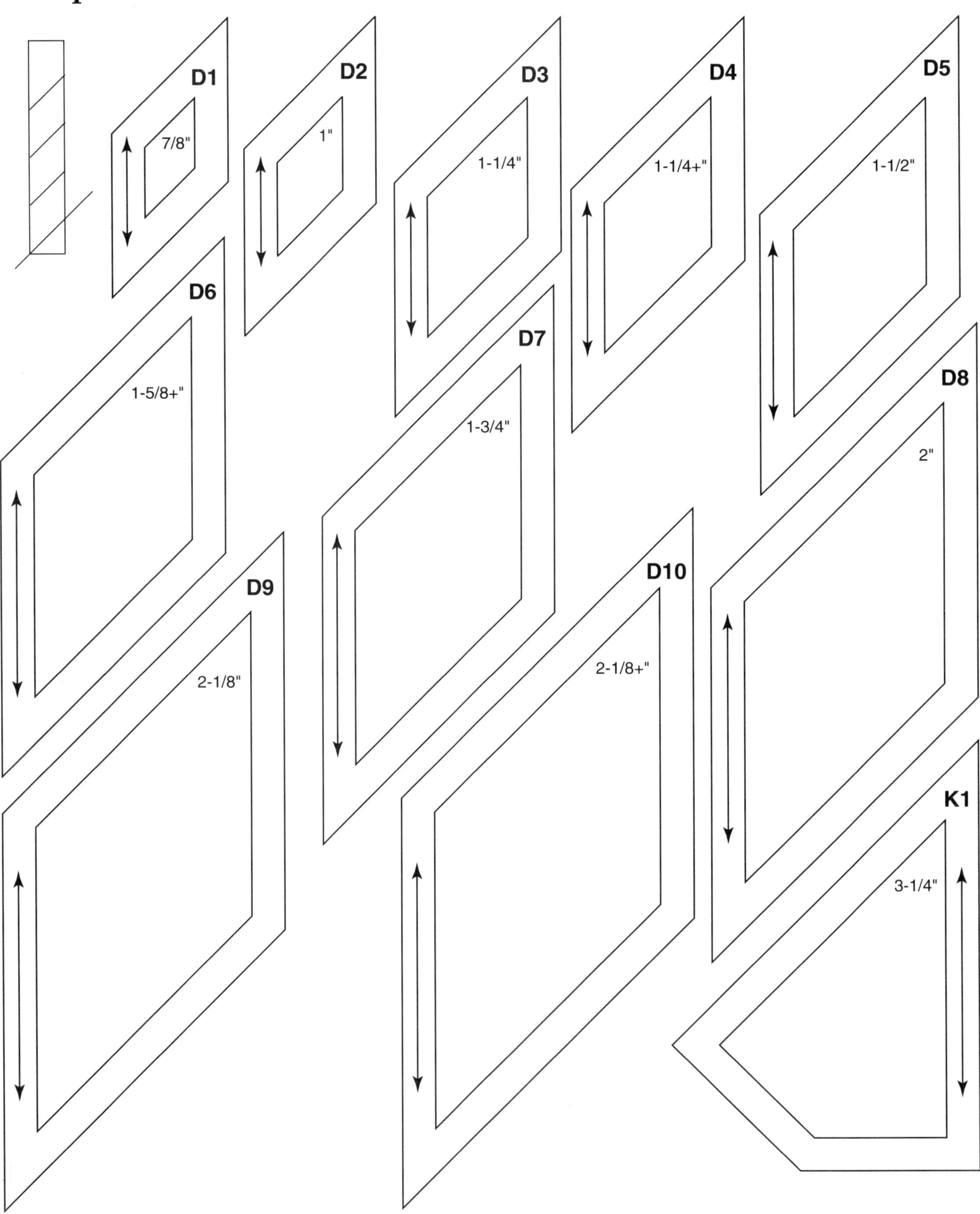

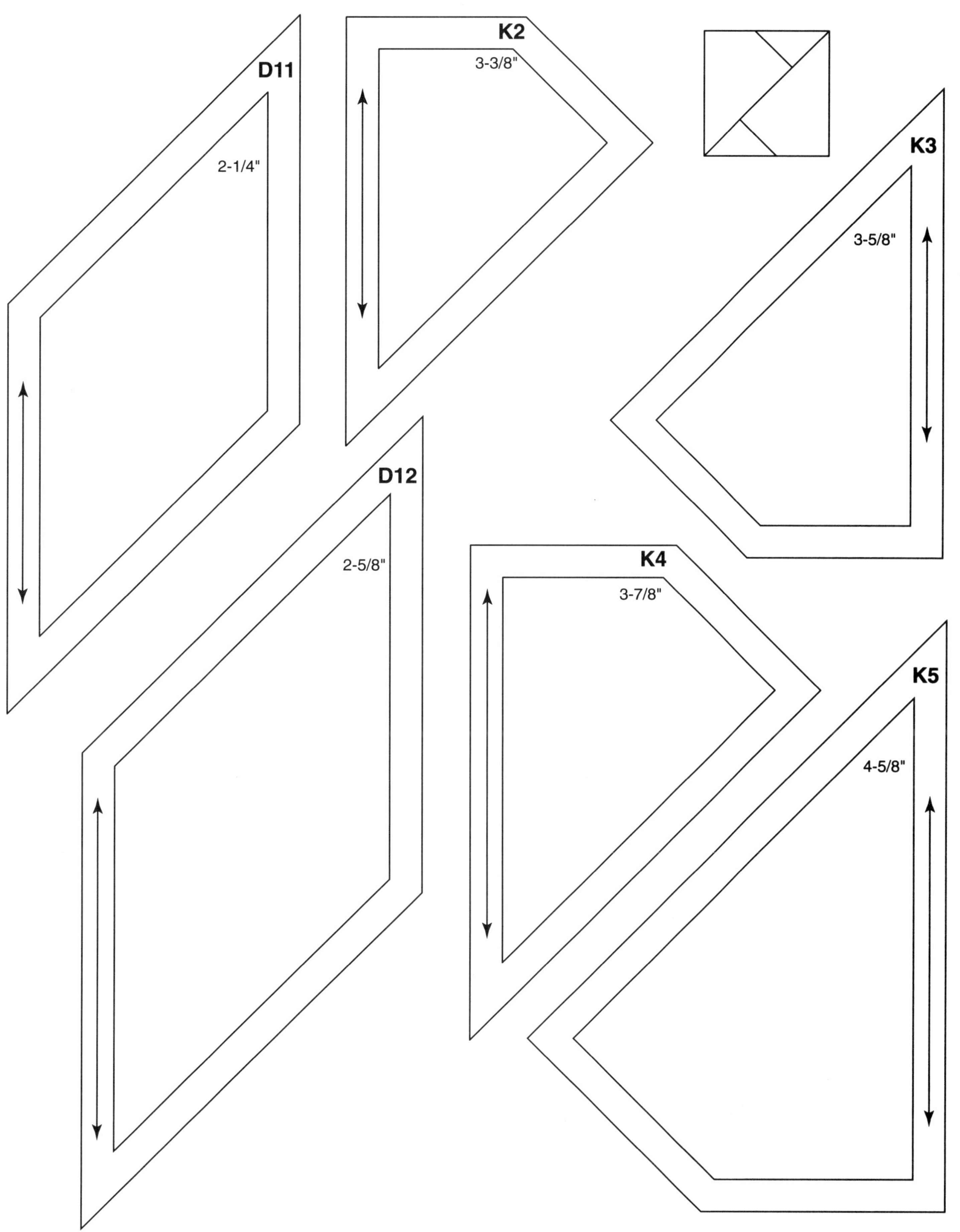

D11
2-1/4"
K2
3-3/8"
K3
3-5/8"
D12
2-5/8"
K4
3-7/8"
K5
4-5/8"

Kites and Octagons

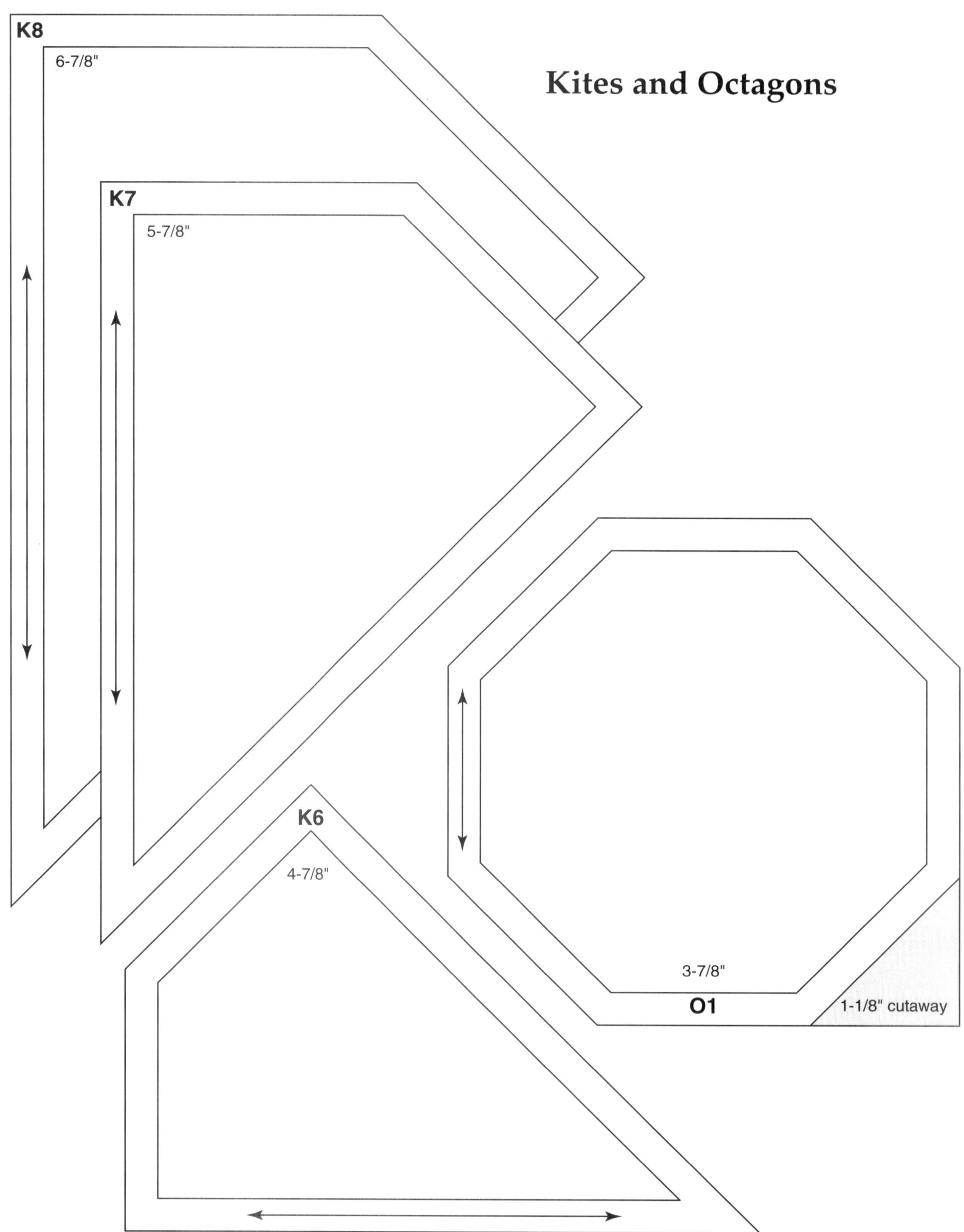

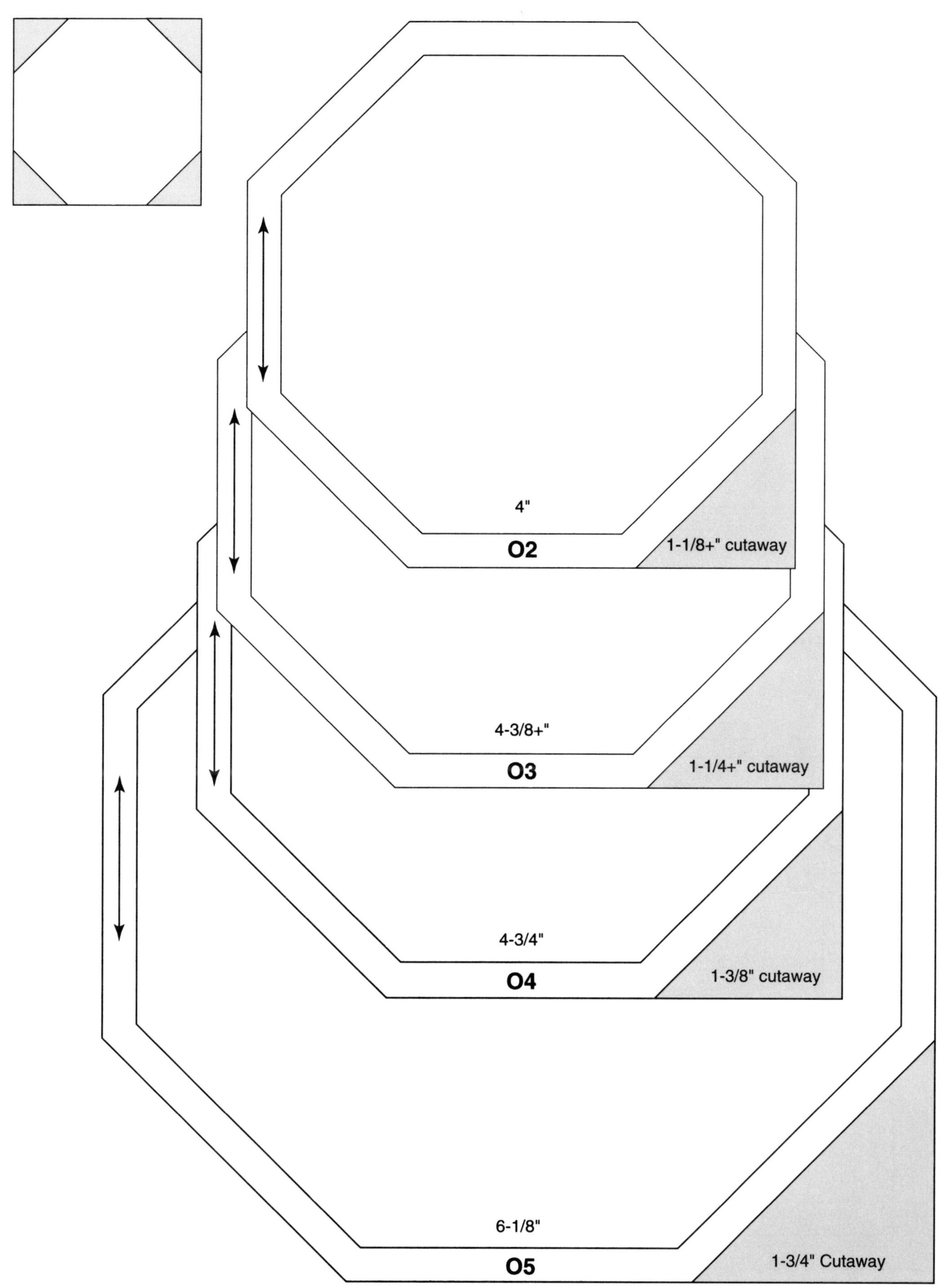
4"
O2
1-1/8+" cutaway
4-3/8+"
O3
1-1/4+" cutaway
4-3/4"
O4
1-3/8" cutaway
6-1/8"
O5
1-3/4" Cutaway

Squares

NT: No Template Given
S11: 6-7/8"
S12: 7-1/4"
S13: 8-5/8"
S14: 11-5/8"

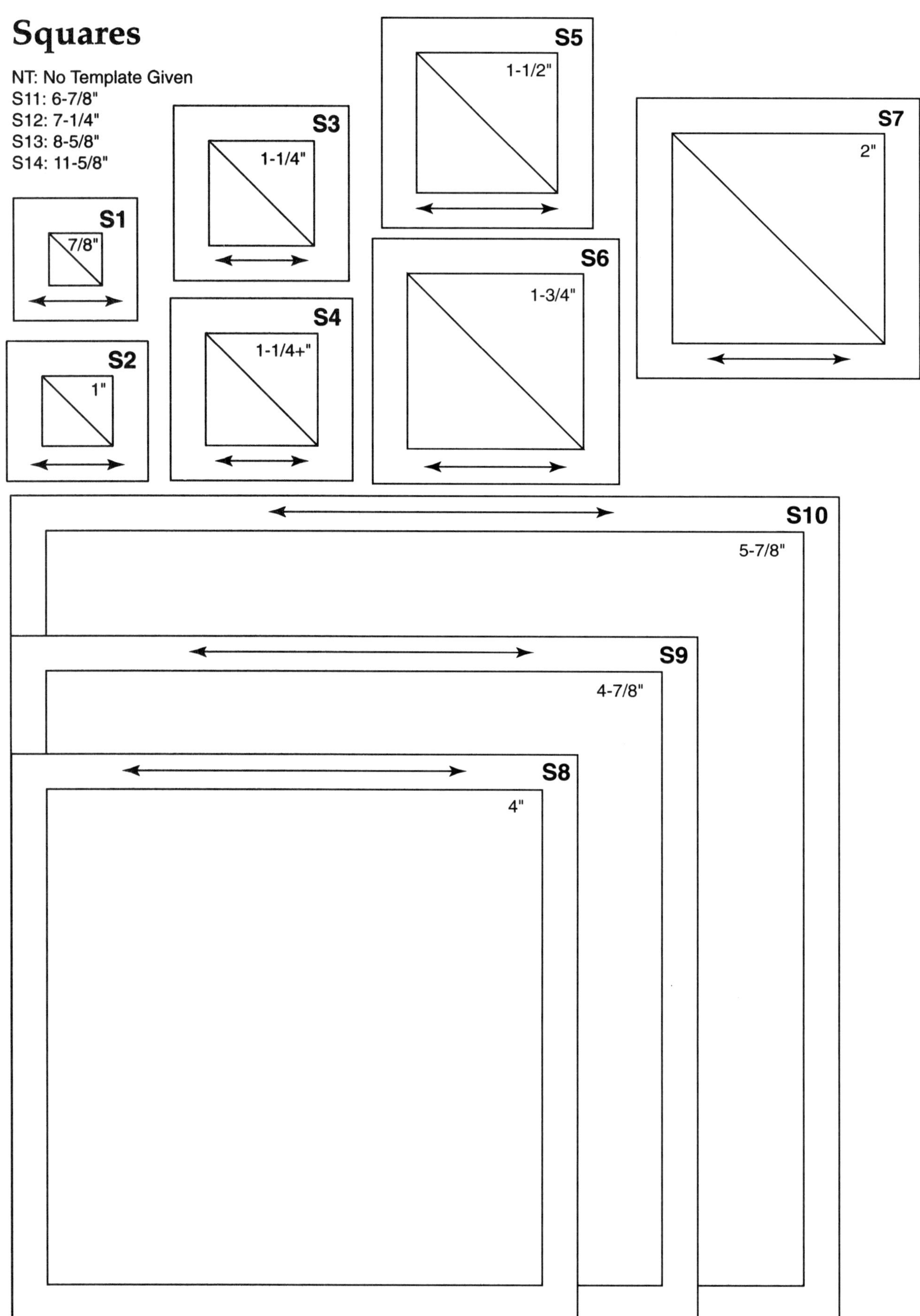

Half-Square Triangles

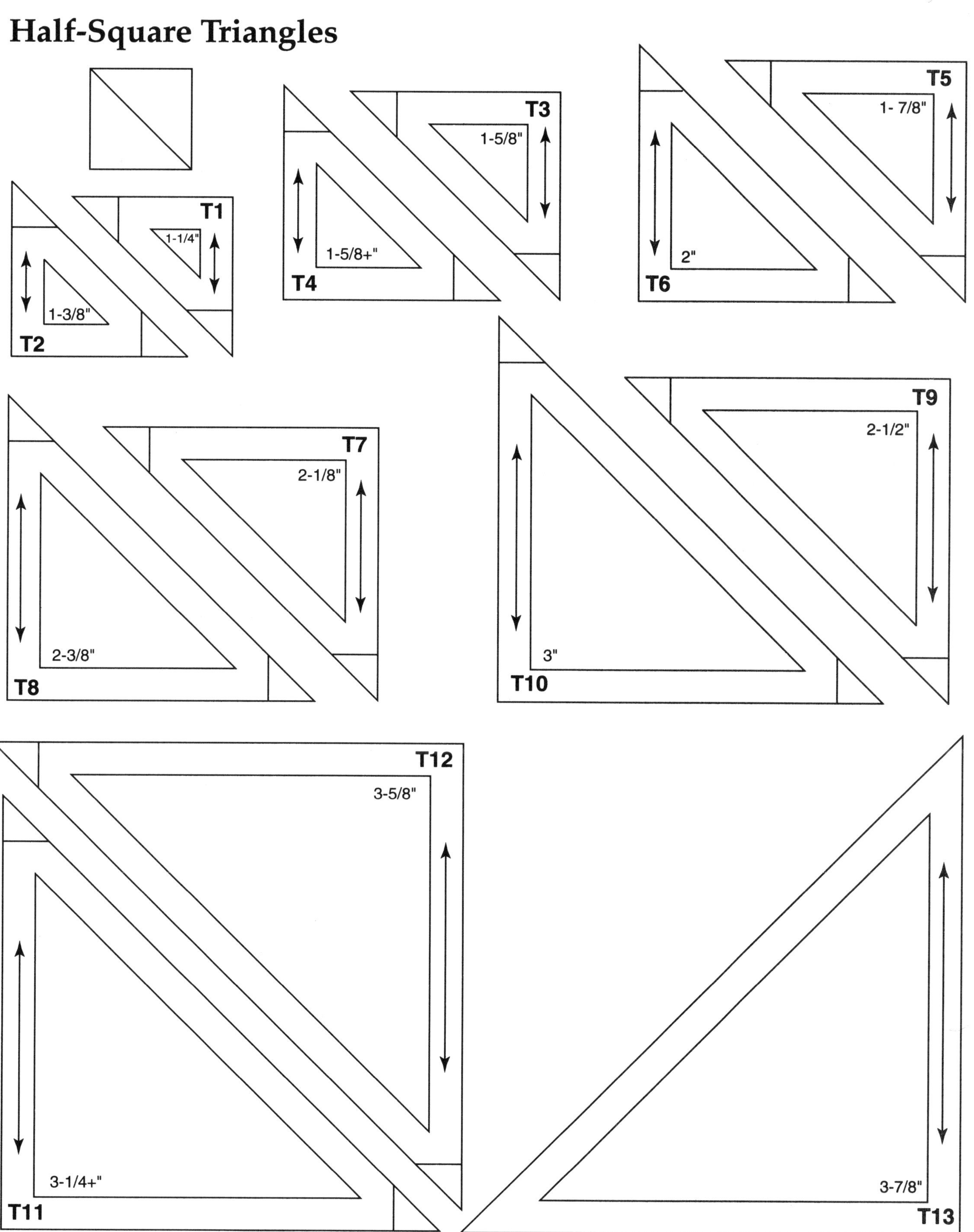

Quarter-Square Triangles

NT: No Template Given
TT8: 7-1/2"
TT9: 7-5/8"
TT10: 8-7/8"
TT11: 10-1/4"
TT12: 10-3/4"
TT13: 10-7/8"
TT14: 12-3/4"
TT15: 17"

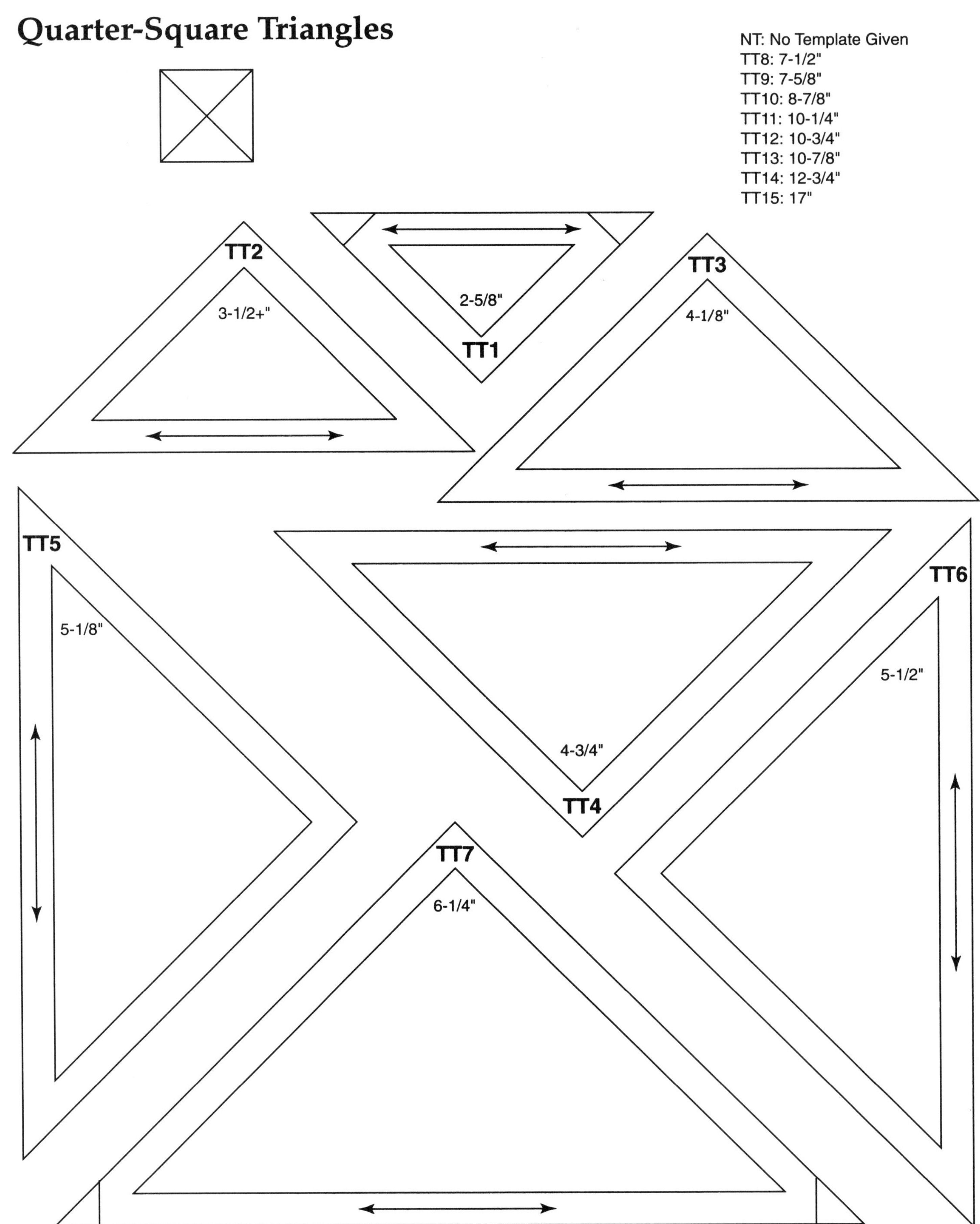

Other Shapes

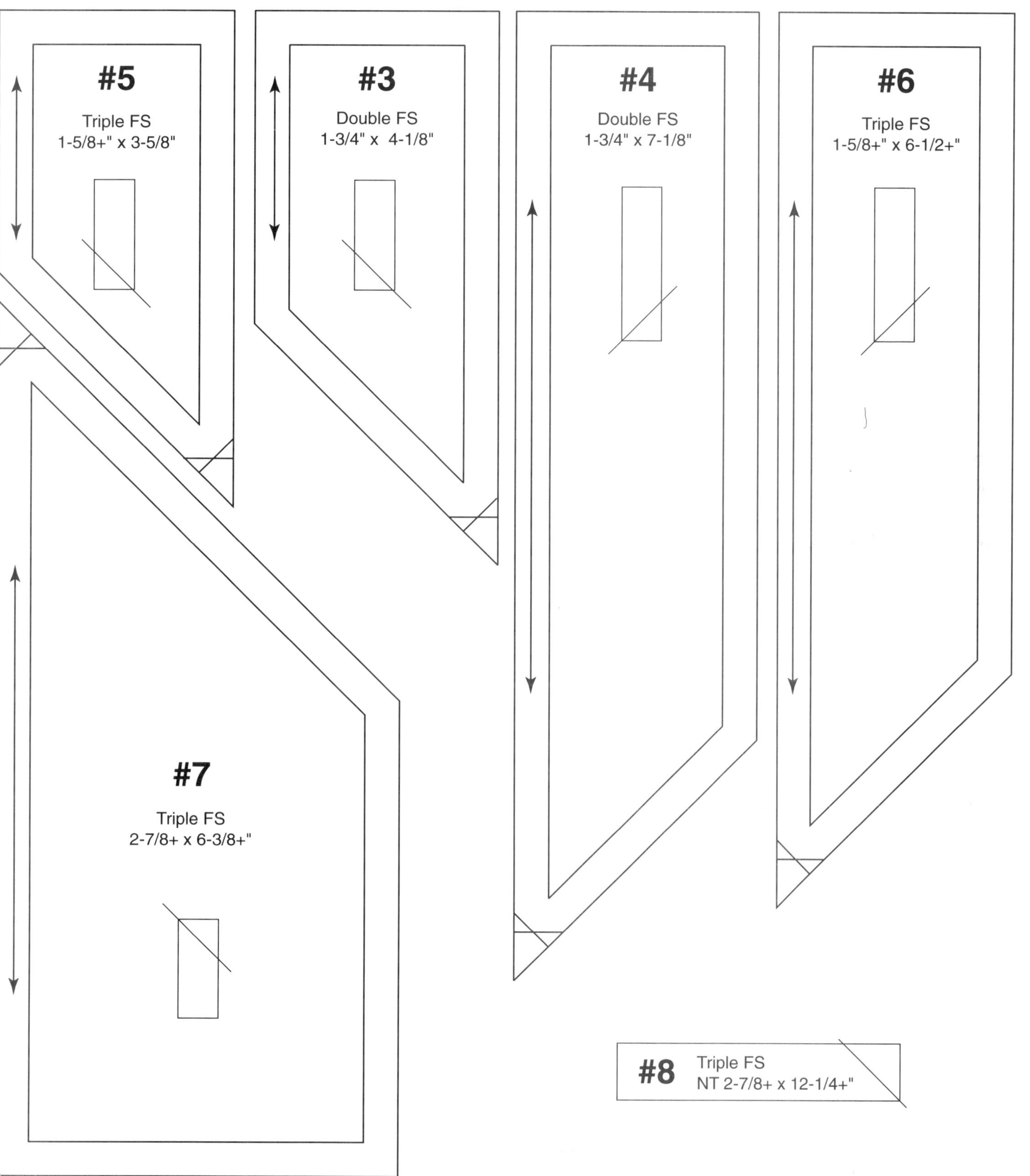

Other Shapes

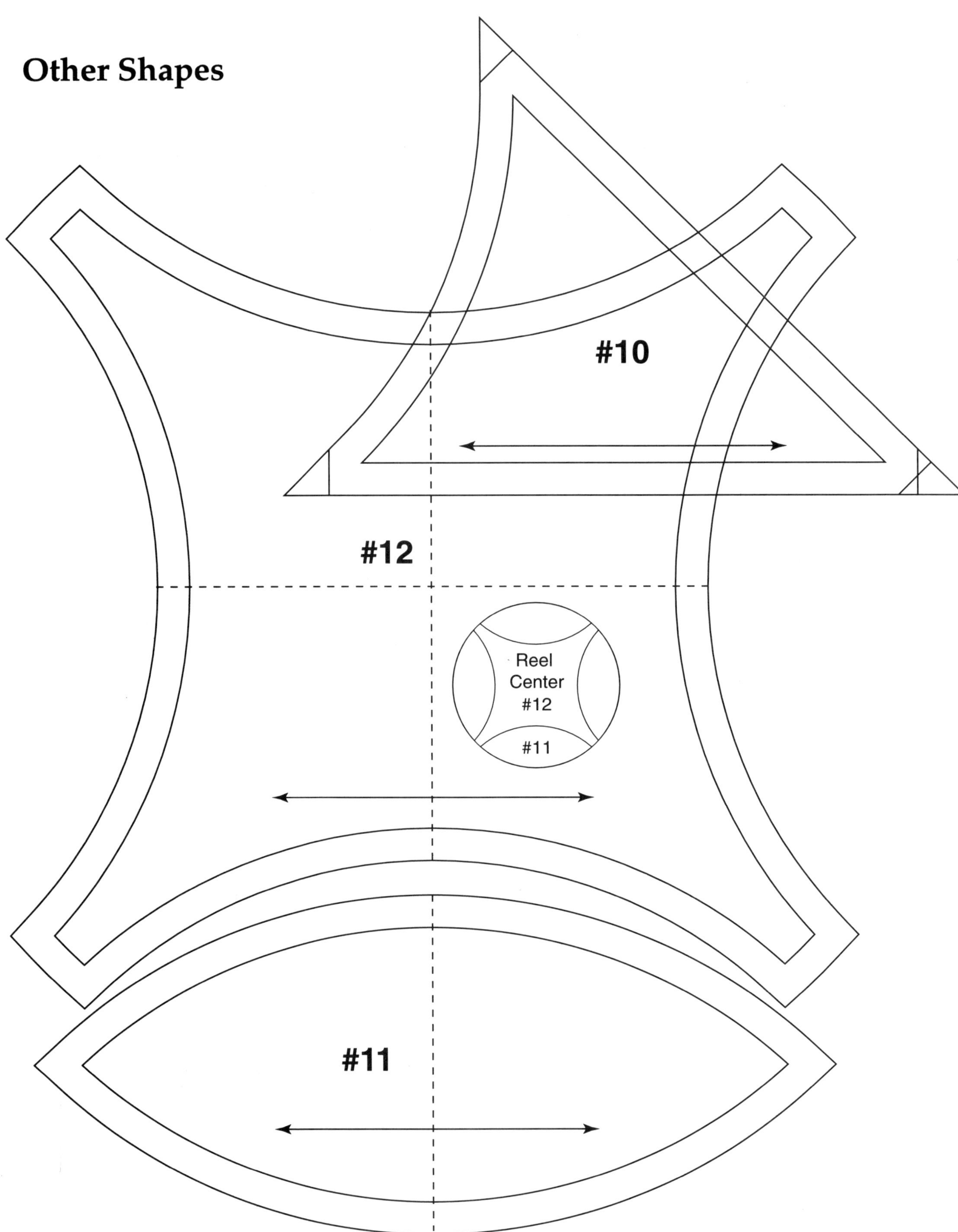